Low Taxes and Small Government

Low Taxes and Small Government

Sam Brownback's Great Experiment in Kansas

Michael A. Smith, Robert J. Grover,
and Rob Catlett

LEXINGTON BOOKS
Lanham • Boulder • New York • London

Published by Lexington Books
An imprint of The Rowman & Littlefield Publishing Group, Inc.
4501 Forbes Boulevard, Suite 200, Lanham, Maryland 20706
www.rowman.com

6 Tinworth Street, London SE11 5AL, United Kingdom

British Library Cataloguing in Publication Information Available

Library of Congress Cataloging-in-Publication Data Available

ISBN 978-1-7936-0482-8 (cloth)
ISBN 978-1-7936-0483-5 (electronic)

Contents

Preface

In 2010 Sam Brownback was elected governor of Kansas on a platform that promised lower taxes and a smaller, efficient state government. Kansans were very familiar with Mr. Brownback because he was a native of the state, graduated from Kansas State University and University of Kansas Law School, served as an attorney practicing in Manhattan (Kansas), and served as Kansas Secretary of Agriculture, U.S. Representative, and U.S. Senator and ran for President of the United States in 2008 before his election as governor in 2010.

His conservative political agenda attracted national attention as he hired Arthur Laffer, the international expert on supply-side economics as a consultant to plan his economic agenda. Mr. Brownback was successful in encouraging the Kansas Legislature to implement a "great experiment" to reduce income taxes as the beginning of a "glide path to zero" income taxes in order to stimulate the economy and shrink the government. He proposed that his Kansas plan would be a fitting model for other states. This book is a case study of the Kansas experiment's implementation and impact.

The authors followed the Kansas Legislature closely during the years 2011–2018. Longtime residents of Kansas, the authors interviewed several legislators, reporters, and knowledgeable observers with backgrounds in economics and Kansas government.

We wish to recognize those who contributed to this book through their willingness to discuss the "great experiment" with us: Paul Davis, Kansas State Representative 2003–2015, Minority Leader 2009–2015, and candidate for governor in 2016; Ed Flentje, retired professor and Director of the Hugo Wall School of Public Affairs at Wichita State University and department heads in the administration of two Kansas governors; Bill Graves, Kansas Secretary of State 1987–1995 and Governor 1995–2003; Martin Hawver, publisher of *Hawver's Capitol Report*, a Kansas legislative and political newsletter, for 25 years; Don Hill, State Representative 2003–2017; Phillip B. Journey, District Court Judge since 2008 and State Representative 2003–2008; Jerry Karr, who served in the Kansas Senate 1983–1998, including several terms as minority leader; Jim Lowther, State Representative 1976–1996; Stephen Koranda, Kansas Public Radio Political Reporter since 2009; and Jeff Longbine, who was elected to the Kansas Senate in 2010 and has served as Senate Vice-President since 2017.

We also thank our friend, Jim Calvert, a retired physics professor at Emporia State University, who contributed to our writing through his observations as a longtime political junkie.

Chapter 1

Sam Brownback's Great Experiment

CHAPTER OVERVIEW

This book describes the low-tax/small-government philosophy that Sam Brownback implemented in Kansas, and we assess its impact on the state's economy and government services. We present Kansas as a case study to demonstrate the impact of this politically popular theory on state government and services—a study that has national significance.

This chapter provides an overview of the book, its purpose, and intended audience. A brief description of each chapter is included.

BOOK OVERVIEW

The low-tax/small-government philosophy is very popular among U.S. conservatives, and Donald Trump included these ideas in his 2016 presidential campaign. California and Massachusetts, among other states, have cut taxes in the past to boost their state's economies. Sam Brownback's 2010 campaign for governor of Kansas was based on this philosophy, and his stated intent during that campaign was to enact a "real experiment" in Kansas to dramatically lower taxes, even eliminating the state income tax ("a glide path to zero"), with the promise of bolstering the state's economy and attracting new businesses and residents—while also shrinking the government.

We introduce Sam Brownback, a Kansas native who rose to leadership as a student at Kansas State University and worked as an attorney in Manhattan, Kansas, before entering state government as Kansas Secretary of Agriculture. He was elected to the U.S. House of Representatives in 1994 and resigned that position after defeating Jill Docking, a Wichita Democrat, for the unexpired term of U.S. Senator Bob Dole. Brownback was reelected in 1998 and again in 2004. In 2010 he was elected governor of Kansas and again in 2014.

We examine Brownback's political philosophy as his career progressed in Washington, DC. We also examine Brownback's adoption of Arthur Laffer's theory of supply-side economics for implementation of his "great experiment," which he described during his campaign for governor. To provide background, we trace the application of supply-side economics from its implementation in Ronald Reagan's administration and analyze the Brownback plan's impact on the Kansas economy, public services, jobs, and families. Newspaper articles, editorials, government documents, writings on economic and political history, and interviews with legislators and other government leaders are used to document the events and analysis.

Brownback has touted his Kansas plan as a model for other states. Government leaders in Missouri, Oklahoma, and Nebraska, and other states have considered adopting plans for lowering taxes to attract business. We provide a case study for government decision makers, students of political science, journalists, economists, and a general audience who follow current politics and government.

We review the implementation of Brownback's plan and the impact on the state's economy and funding of public services. In so doing, we report the reactions of the state's columnists, economists, other government officials, and citizens as the governor's plan was implemented.

Finally, we present our analysis of the policies implemented and their impact on state government and services, the economy, public education, and the business environment. Implications for other states are presented.

WHY THIS BOOK IS IMPORTANT

Politics in the United States has witnessed an escalating movement to conservatism. The Reagan presidency ushered in a brand of conservatism not witnessed before at the presidential level. Reagan promoted to his cabinet a number of conservatives, including Donald Rumsfeld and Dick Cheney, who had first gained prominence in the Gerald Ford administration, and these leaders in turn brought in a new brand of economics that became known as *supply-side economics*. At the core of this philosophy is an economic system that opposes the Keynesian philosophy of progressives. According to supply-side economists, smaller government, lower taxes, and incentives for business and investors are the foundation for economic growth. Consequently, laws and policies are passed that support this philosophical stance.

This book provides background for the political philosophy behind supply-side economics and traces its historical development in this country. With Sam Brownback's declaration that he planned to implement a "real experiment" in Kansas that would provide a "shot of adrenalin" to the state's economy, Kansas became a laboratory to test the concepts behind supply-side economics. Brownback hired Arthur Laffer, acknowledged as the co-founder with Robert A. Mundell of supply-side economics, as a consultant to help his administration plan a strategy for this experiment.

Other states have followed suit, although some began implementing low-tax/small-government plans before Kansas began its efforts in 2011. Candidates for state and national governments have echoed the mantra of supply-side economics, and many have been elected to state legislatures, governorships, and Congress. Kansas has been touted by Governor Brownback as a model for other states. During the presidential election of 2016, Republican candidate Donald Trump proposed similar policies for his presidency.

What were the results of the Brownback Great Experiment in Kansas, and what are the implications for other states? The analysis of the Kansas experience is of profound importance for the nation.

AUDIENCE

This book is written for political science faculty and students, politicians, government leaders, political reporters and analysts, and political strategists who are dealing with these issues on a daily basis. We also anticipate a general audience that follows American politics—political "junkies" who like to talk politics around the water cooler and to share their views on social media. National media have chronicled the Kansas "experiment," and both a national and international audience is probable.

CHAPTER DESCRIPTIONS

Chapter 2 traces Sam Brownback's political career from his student leadership at Kansas State University to the U.S. House of Representatives, U.S. Senate, and run for the presidency before he was elected Kansas governor. During his campaign for governor in 2010, Brownback promised an efficient state government and an economic upturn.

Chapter 3 suggests that Brownback's election as governor was part of a national movement to conservatism and the application of libertarian ideals. After his election as governor, Brownback hired Arthur Laffer, recognized as the cofounder of supply-side economics, as a consultant to help him plan and implement the "great experiment" of cutting taxes, boosting the economy, and shrinking government. During the 2012 legislative session, Brownback led the effort in the Kansas Legislature to pass key legislation making major changes in the tax structure.

Chapter 4 explores the low-tax/small-government ideology. An overview of supply-side economics is provided, with a focus on Arthur Laffer's theory (the "Laffer Curve") as applied to U.S. politics from Ronald Reagan's presidency to its application in Kansas.

Chapter 5 follows years three and four of Brownback's first term, which saw the passage of more legislation to cut taxes that continued the "glide path to zero" income taxes. Brownback and conservative leaders ran effective campaigns to oust moderates in the Republican Party who opposed his plan. Media accounts and interviews of political leaders document implementation of the Brownback plan.

Chapter 6 describes how the 2014 election brought to the public the impact of Brownback's legislative program, and those issues are analyzed. Reelected by a slim margin in 2014, Brownback received support from voters and a conservative majority in both houses of the legislature to continue his low-tax small-government program. This chapter recounts the legislation and issues prominent in years 2015–2016.

Chapter 7 follows Brownback's governorship following the 2016 election and the policy changes that resulted from an election that brought more moderate legislators to the Kansas Legislature. The unwinding of the "great experiment" is described.

Chapter 8 uses state and federal government data and analyses by economists to assess the impact of Brownback's programs on Kansas and the reaction of segments of the population. Public education, human services, the economy and government services, in general, are examined; assessments by state leaders, economists, and political science experts are included.

Chapter 9 provides an analysis of Kansas as a model for other states and for the United States. The chapter summarizes the impact of the "great experiment" on the Kansas economy, state budget, public services, state infrastructure, and health care system. The authors provide their rationale for the experiment's failure to achieve Brownback's stated goals.

Chapter 10, the "Afterword," describes the aftermath of the Great Experiment after Brownback left the state and a new governor was elected. Other states have tried lowering taxes, and the results in Missouri, Louisiana, and Texas are described briefly. Governor Brownback often compared the Kansas Experiment to the low-tax structure employed in Texas.

The bibliography is a listing of related books cited in the chapters.

DEFINITIONS

The following terms are part of the discussion throughout the book, and broad definitions are provided below. We are using popularized definitions and applications; quotation marks identify definitions from *Merriam-Webster's Dictionary* online (https://www.merriam-webster.com).

Conservatism—"a political philosophy based on tradition and social stability, stressing established institutions, and preferring gradual development to abrupt change; *specifically*: such a philosophy calling for lower taxes, limited government regulation of business and investing, a strong national defense, and individual financial responsibility for personal needs (such as retirement income or health-care coverage)."

Evangelical—"of, relating to, or being in agreement with the Christian gospel especially as it is presented in the four Gospels."

Federalism—"the distribution of power in an organization (such as a government) between a central authority and the constituent units."

Fundamentalist—"a movement or attitude stressing strict and literal adherence to a set of basic principles."

"Great Experiment"—Sam Brownback's term for his plan to cut taxes a boost the Kansas economy. The term was used during his campaign for governor and was applied throughout his two terms as governor of Kansas.

Keynesian—"the economic theories and programs ascribed to John M. Keynes and his followers; *specifically*: the advocacy of monetary and fiscal programs by government to increase employment and spending."

Laffer Curve—a diagram shaped like a normal curve that is intended to show the relationship between tax rates and tax revenues. See chapter 4 for a more detailed explanation.

Liberalism—"a political philosophy based on belief in progress, the essential goodness of the human race, and the autonomy of the individual and standing for the protection of political and civil liberties; *specifically*: such a philosophy that considers government as a crucial instrument for amelioration of social inequities (such as those involving race, gender, or class)."

Libertarian—"a person who upholds the principles of individual liberty especially of thought and action."

Moderate—"professing or characterized by political or social beliefs that are not extreme."

Populist—"a believer in the rights, wisdom, or virtues of the common people."

Pro-choice—favoring the legalization of abortion. Providing individuals an opportunity to choose to have an abortion.

Progressive—"of, relating to, or characterized by progress; making use of or interested in new ideas, findings, or opportunities."

Supply-side economics—"a theory that reducing taxes especially for rich people will lead to an improved economy." See chapter 4, for a discussion of the evolution of supply-side economics and its application in the United States.

REFERENCE

Merriam-Webster Online Dictionary. 2015. Springfield, MA: Merriam-Webster, Inc. https://www.merriam-webster.com.

Chapter 2

From God's Senator to Glide Path

INTRODUCTION: HE NEVER WAVERED

As a U.S. senator, Sam Brownback identified himself very strongly by his religious faith. In his public comments, his behavior, and his autobiography, Brownback stressed his faith as the core of his decision-making—and his electoral coalition. He defeated his primary and general election opponents to become a U.S. senator in 1996 by stressing his faith-based appeals to churches, Christian homeschoolers, the anti-abortion movement, and the others collectively known as the "religious right" (Scheiber 2006). As a senator, he stressed conservative positions on social issues like abortion rights and same-sex marriage, and spearheaded a drive to block one of George W. Bush's more moderate Supreme Court nominees, Harriet Miers, whom he argued did not have enough experience for the job (*ibid.*). Skeptical commentators suggested it was, in fact, because Miers may not have voted to overturn the landmark abortion rights ruling *Roe v Wade*. Also stressing his faith, Brownback crossed party lines on other issues, including his outspoken advocacy for human rights in Darfur, Sudan, along with bills increasing penalties for human trafficking (Brownback 2007). Brownback and his staff were even drafting an immigration reform bill including a path to citizenship together with Senator Ted Kennedy and his staff, before it was derailed by post-9/11 politics (Camerini and Robertson 2010). Later, after a tumultuous Senate confirmation vote, Brownback resigned his governorship a year early to take a new job as U.S. Ambassador for Religious Freedom in the Trump administration.

Why, then, did a former Senator who identified first and foremost with his religious faith become the driver of a drastic tax-cutting experiment? Once labeled "God's Senator" (Sharlet 2006), today his name is permanently bonded to the "glide path to zero." Of course, modern conservatism does blend small-government, low-tax themes with an emphasis on traditional values. Essentially, the value system proposes to reduce government's role in providing education, direct payments, and social services, replacing it with a bigger role for families (particularly traditional ones headed by married heterosexual parents), churches, religiously affiliated nonprofits, and the like. Thus, as a conservative, Brownback's positions were ideologically consistent. Yet questions remain about the shift in emphasis. His written work, speeches, and previous career would lead an observer to expect a governorship tightly focused on rejecting same-sex marriage (despite a U.S. Supreme Court ruling), restricting abortion in any way possible, and seeking new opportunities to challenge *Roe v Wade*, while trying to find ways to encourage marriage. Indeed, Brownback's administration did all these things, particularly in the renamed Department of Children and Families, headed for several years by Brownback appointee Phyllis Gilmore.

Still, as governor, Brownback himself was primarily consumed with the other aspect of conservatism—the more libertarian one—cutting taxes. Instead of being remembered first and foremost as an advocate of faith in the public square, traditional families, and criminalizing abortion, Brownback identified himself with the tax cut early on, and never wavered. To most observers, his reasons for doing this remain obscure, the explanations largely a matter of speculation. In public utterances, Brownback never budged from his claim that the tax cuts were starting to work and that the state's budget problems were due to the downturn in the agricultural, oil, gas, and manufacturing sectors, not the tax cut.

Did Brownback pray about this? Did he feel called to defend the tax cut? Was it part of a larger plan to defund public institutions so that, for example, parents would opt for Christian private schools or homeschooling instead of public schools? Did he place too much trust in his inner circle of advisors? Did he truly believe that state-specific economic downturns were to blame for the budget shortfall? Were political players, like Kansas natives Charles and David Koch—both libertarian capitalists who are not particularly religious—the ones driving this behind the scenes with Brownback as their front man? Speculation runs rampant, but observers may never truly get definitive answers to any of these questions. Brownback plays his cards close to his vest with any question save the one that lies at the core of his public life: his religious faith.

On the tax cut, Brownback was indeed very consistent in his response to critics. No matter how many times he was asked, no matter the context, he could be counted on to answer that the state's budget problems were not due to the tax cut but rather to downturns in the farm, oil and gas, and manufacturing industries. Critics like former Budget Director Duane Goossen countered with cross-state regional comparisons showing that, for example, Iowa and Nebraska did not suffer the same budget crisis during this period (Goossen 2016). Brownback never acknowledged Goossen's responses and instead stuck to his explanation, even when being questioned by the U.S. senators before taking up his new ambassador job. Economic downturns—not necessarily seen to the same degree in the rest of the country—caused the budget shortfall, according to Brownback, and that was all there was to say about that.

This chapter features a brief, political biography of Sam Brownback, from his early political activities including being a Future Farmers of America president, to his seven years as Governor of Kansas, where his name was indelibly linked with a single act: signing a tax cut bill in 2014 that radically altered the state's budget and set in motion one of the most aggressive experiments in supply-side economics ever tried in a U.S. state. In the end, though, few definitive answers emerge to the central question: *Why did he do it?* Why did a governor so closely identified with his religious faith invest nearly all of his political capital in the libertarian aspect of conservatism, which had not, previously, been his focus or his passion? Why no course correction? Through review of the extensive writings on Brownback during his brief run for U.S. President, along with multiple interviews (but not one with Brownback himself, who declined), and a close reading of the aforementioned autobiography, insights are gleaned—but ultimately, the only one who may ever know why Brownback took the actions he did, and steadfastly refused to change course, may be the former governor himself.

A CASE STUDY IN CONTRADICTIONS: PRISONS

One of the greatest puzzles of Brownback's signature act was that it seemed to undermine his own, self-identified priorities. Prisons are a case in point. In *From Power to Purpose*, Brownback wrote,

> In 1980, there were over five hundred thousand men and women in federal, state, and local prisons and jails; today that number stands at 2.1 million. Statistics show that two-thirds of those who are released from prison will be arrested and again be incarcerated at some point in their lives. The statistics are very clear: we have a problem with our prison system that needs to be addressed.
>
> There's hope in the midst of these dire statistics, and this hope can be found in programs that not only nurture education and job-training skills, but nurture the soul of the individual as well. (p. 70)

Ten years after he wrote those words, after years of short staffing and budget cuts, a riot broke out at Kansas' Norton Correctional Facility. Fires were set, windows smashed, and staff offices occupied. Inmates wielded homemade weapons, and syringes were missing from the medical facilities. The problem stemmed from the housing of maximum-security inmates at this medium-security facility in preparation for renovations to the state's decrepit facility at Lansing (Lowry and Londberg 2017). Lansing, in turn, is one of the oldest state prisons still in use and has years of deferred maintenance problems. It is located near the iconic federal penitentiary at Leavenworth.

Back at Norton, analysts also traced the problem to overcrowding and lack of staff, both due to the budget cuts. Lowry and Londberg wrote, "Single cells have been converted to double cells and doubles to quadruples, the [unnamed] officer said." They also noted that the facility had 17 staff vacancies while Lansing had 109 vacancies. After years of low pay and difficulty recruiting officers, Brownback had recently signed a bill to increase it in hopes of filling the vacancies, but it was too late to avert this riot.

Brownback's handling of another corrections issue is equally puzzling. Eight years after specifically addressing the need and importance of programs that "nurture education and job-training skills" in his book, Brownback used these same programs as a bargaining chip in 2015. That year featured the longest Kansas Legislature session in the state's history, to date, as lawmakers wrestled with tax proposals that would partially close the budget hole caused (according to most observers, though not Brownback himself) by the 2012 income tax cuts. Brownback supported, and the Legislature belatedly passed, a bill to raise the state's sales tax. Cuts to prison programs were threatened if it did not pass. Reporting in the *Hutchinson News*, reporter Kelton Brooks (2015) wrote, "Inmate rehabilitation programs and staff could be eliminated in Hutchinson, Larned and other Kansas prisons if the Legislature can't pass tax increases to balance the state budget."

Quoting Kansas Department of Corrections spokesman Adam Pfannenstiel, Brooks added that even before the proposed new cuts, "Four of Kansas' correction facilities are currently facing 15 to 20 percent vacancies."

In the end, the sales tax increase did pass, partially—and only partially—restoring revenues, but also making Kansas' tax on groceries one of the highest in the nation. The worst cuts were averted, but the staffing shortages persisted. The Norton riot was two years later.

All of this seems particularly odd given a theme that our interviewees stressed again and again—Brownback's sincerity. For example, Kansas judge and ex-state senator Phil Journey (2018) stated in our interview that "I've known Sam since he was Secretary of Agriculture, alright?" His take on the governor's character? "One thing about Brownback that's different from a lot of politicians is that he thinks one thing, says the same thing and does the same," Journey said. "That's not most politicians."

Why the apparent reversal on prisons, then?

Perhaps it was not a reversal at all. One clue may lie in Brownback's writings:

> Yes, I had been student body president, national vice president of the FFA, an attorney, secretary of agriculture, a White House Fellow, and now I was one of the leaders of the Republican Revolution in Congress. I had done all that. But what did it mean? I was just building my "City of Man."
>
> That was St. Augustine's term for it in his classic work *The City of God*. When your only frame of reference is limited to the finite physical world, you're not living by any higher standard. You're living in the temporal and profane conceits of your own heart. I was doing pretty well at it, I thought. But all of that came crashing down, and I finally just gave up. One night I got down on my knees and said, "OK, Lord, that's it. I give up. It's all Yours. This life is Yours, and You can do whatever You like." (Brownback, Ch. 2)

Brownback ends the earlier quote by stating that prison programs must "nurture the soul as well." In the following passages of his book, Brownback extols the virtues of Prison Ministries, the project spearheaded by former Nixon administration Watergate operative Charles Colson, who converted to evangelical Christianity while in prison himself. Brownback praised the programs and denounced organizations like the American Civil Liberties Union (ACLU) and Americans United for the Separation of Church and State (AU) for suing the state of Iowa to end the program.

The success of Prison Ministries is in fact mixed (Paynter 2004), but this did not stop Brownback and other Christian conservatives from being their enthusiastic advocates. Given the quote above, perhaps this former God's Senator placed no value on prison programs that were located in the "finite, physical world." Brownback's exaltations were reserved only for Prison Ministries—only for programs that combined faith with the other, secular goals of job training and avoiding recidivism. Re-analysis of Prison Ministries' breathless claims indicates that they often cherry-pick their results by excluding those who drop out of the program, even if they drop out after being released. More rigorous re-analyses have found that the results are in fact mixed, when compared with the general prison population—one study even found that the recidivism rate was *higher* than for those in the general prison population (*ibid.*). Interestingly, Paynter's exposé also noted that the program entices state policymakers with budgetary relief: Prison Ministries offers to take on many of the costs of housing the inmates, even the secular aspects, for the first few years, so as to get a toehold in the state prison systems. As far as Brownback's opinions go, he concludes that section of his book with the expected, Christian Conservative denunciations of the ACLU and AU for suing to stop the program on First Amendment grounds.

In sum, the best surmise may be that prison conditions and budget cuts were meaningless to Brownback unless they were connected to faith. Like his hero St. Augustine, Brownback had little interest in the finite, physical world. Prison Ministries is a program to be extolled, but the secular aspects of the state correctional system were of little interest. Brownback continued his book's passage on prisons,

> Today, in prisons where mentoring programs and faith-based initiatives are operating, the recidivism rate is under 10 percent. Why? Because while the body may be locked up, the soul of the inmate is free, and the freedom of the soul can lead to a reformation of life. (p. 72)

The researchers cited by Paynter would contest Brownback's statistics, but no matter. The point is, in faith, the prisoner's soul must be freed from the body. But for that, prisons are just another budgetary headache—one that dogged Brownback throughout his governorship.

BEGINNINGS: A PUBLIC RELATIONS MAN AT THE DEPARTMENT OF AGRICULTURE

Like a lot of future politicians, Sam Brownback had a leadership role when he was young, serving as President of the Kansas Future Farmers of America while he was still a teenager (Brownback 2007). After law school, while he was working as an attorney in Manhattan, Kansas, Brownback was tapped to be Secretary of Agriculture in the administration of Republican Governor Mike Hayden.

Hayden was a moderate Republican, at a time when the Republican Party was showing its first fissures, just beginning to split into rival factions. In the late 1980s and early 1990s, when Hayden served, an insurgent group of conservative Republicans out of Johnson County (suburban Kansas City) was becoming increasingly restive with the moderate tone of the state's dominant GOP (Loomis 1993). Kansas moderate Republican candidates would generally shy away from social issues such as abortion rights, which had entered the national stage after the 1973 *Roe v. Wade* United States Supreme Court ruling. Kansas moderates continued ruling in their same tradition of limited, but competent government that had particularly gained ground under the administration of Governor Bob Bennett in the mid-1970s. In fact, in twentieth-century Kansas history, there were times when Democrats, such as Governor George Docking, ran to the right of Republicans such as Bennett. Hayden was very much a Republican in this moderate tradition. He hailed from rural Kansas, was noted for his folksy demeanor, and made occasional gaffes (*ibid*). He certainly sounded like a Republican stressing small-government themes, but what Hayden presided over was largely a maintenance of the state's good, if limited, government tradition.

Brownback joined the Hayden administration without a pronounced ideological agenda. His leadership as a teenager in the FFA seemed to prepare him well for this job, and his legal background was another plus. At this time, the Kansas Department of Agriculture was viewed by many as a captive of the interest groups which it was supposed to be regulating, particularly the Farm Bureau. As a matter of fact, just a few years later, the court would rule that the state must restructure the Department of Agriculture, because the current structure allowed in the very interest groups that it was supposed to be regulating to appoint its members (Scott 1995).

Not a lot is on record about Brownback's service as Kansas Secretary of Agriculture, coming as it does before his religious conversion and his most notable public accomplishments. However, one notable exception is former Kansas senator Jerry Karr, a Democrat from Emporia. Karr remembered Brownback's service in this role, and he told interviewers that the future governor was a showman, saying,

> Brownback became Secretary of Agriculture in the mid-80s. He was selected by the Ag Council, made up of representatives from counties that had large memberships in Farm Bureau. That's the first time I met him . . .
>
> It was in the mid-[19]80s when everything was going wrong in the agriculture sector. So he set up a committee on his own to do a report on what we needed to do to promote rural Kansas. I happened to be on that committee. Farm Bureau wasn't too impressed with him doing that . . .
>
> He took the job just to do public promotion of agriculture in the state—not anything to do with the running of the department. When it became apparent that the department was having troubles, particularly in the weights and measures because they handle all of the scales and grocery stores and filling stations and things like that. It was sad that Agriculture internally had been so inbred; there were problems . . .
>
> They had about 60 major laws or regulations and restaurants were under the inspection of the Department of Agriculture. The chemical division, certifying seed, and weights and measures were some of the many areas. But he got engaged in doing his PR but not running the department because there were vested interests that were running it and they didn't want him even messing with it. And he was willing not to mess with it. (Karr 2018)

In sum, according to Karr, Brownback liked to give speeches and do the public relations part of the job, more than he did the day-to-day administrative part. The policy of just letting interest groups run the department would soon generate a court ruling, mandating that the Department be restructured.

In a sense, this may have been a harbinger of things to come.

A TERM IN THE HOUSE: FROM NO CONTRACT TO NEW FEDERALIST

Brownback's next major political move was to seek a seat in the U.S. Congressional district which encompassed Topeka, part of college-town Lawrence, and the rural southeastern part of the state, which used to vote more Democratic than did other parts of rural Kansas (Peirce and Hagstrom 1983). That congressional district has been served by Democrat Jim Slattery for several terms until Slattery decided to seek the governorship. In 1994, Slattery vacated the seat for his gubernatorial run, which he did not win. Interestingly, in *From Power to Purpose*, Brownback wrote that Slattery contacted him and told him that he was not running for reelection, hinting that Brownback may wish to seek the seat himself. In the end, Slattery lost while Brownback won, flipping this swing district as part of the Republican wave election in 1994.

Brownback was one of only a few GOP challengers not to sign Newt Gingrich's "Contract with America" in 1994. The "Contract" was a series of small-government, socially conservative campaign promises which were designed to get the Republican challengers in that year running on similar themes, effectively nationalizing the elections, rather than running elections as largely local, in-district affairs, as has been the longstanding practice. Republican leadership like Gingrich had decided that localizing elections played into the hands of Democrats. After all, it was Democratic Speaker of the House Tip O'Neill who had famously said "all politics is local."

Brownback, however, had reservations about the "Contract." In *From Power to Purpose*, he stated his reason, if vaguely: he thought the "Contract's" proposed reforms to public welfare programs could be "done differently." At any rate, Brownback pulled off the win, and changes were in store during his single term in the U.S. House of Representatives.

Brownback may have appeared to be tacking moderate by refusing to sign the "Contract," but things changed quickly when he got to Washington. Unable to secure other leadership posts, Brownback discovered a group called the New Federalists, a small-government group of newly elected Republican members in the House (Brownback 2007). Brownback rose quickly to leadership in this group, which took highly confrontational positions, pushing the already-conservative Gingrich further to the right. In particular, the New Federalists were noted for their advocacy of a confrontational approach toward President Bill Clinton, pushing Gingrich toward the government shutdowns for which the Republican Congress became known. Conventional wisdom holds that these government shutdowns generally played into Clinton's hands, not Gingrich's, as measured by approval polls of both during the incidents, plus the 1998 midterm elections. Nevertheless, the New Federalists, including Brownback, were strong advocates of this confrontational approach, challenging a sitting Democratic president and insisting on measures to reduce the size and scope of the federal government.

A TURN TO THE RIGHT: THE '96 SENATE RUN

Brownback's term in the U.S. House was to be his only one. In 1996, an opportunity opened up: one that at first seemed a long shot. However, Brownback was determined. Senator Robert Dole had been Kansas' senior U.S. senator for quite some time. Rising to be the Majority Leader of the Senate, Dole was a major power broker and antagonist of President Clinton. Earlier, also as Majority Leader, Dole had been a key ally of President Reagan. Dole made the run for President in 1996, securing the Republican nomination to challenge Clinton. Dole resigned his Senate seat to campaign. This created a vacancy.

Both of Kansas's Senate seats thus appeared on the ballot in the same year, because the other seat was scheduled for an election on the six-year cycle. For the full six-year term, rural "Big First" District Congressman Pat Roberts easily won the seat when longtime Kansas junior senator Nancy Landon Kassebaum retired. The hot race was the other one—the one to complete Dole's term. Conventional wisdom was betting on Sheila Frahm, a former lieutenant governor who had been appointed by Governor Bill Graves to serve temporarily when Dole resigned. Graves, a strong moderate, supported Frahm enthusiastically. Brownback's run against Frahm crystallized along the moderate-conservative division that had come to define the Kansas Republican Party.

Before the 1990s, the chair of the Kansas Republican Party would typically be a very strong supporter of the state's Republican governors. Not so this time. The moderate Graves was strongly opposed by GOP Chairman David Miller, so much so that Miller resigned his post in order to run for governor in the primary against Graves. In a personal interview, Graves expressed his disappointment at Miller's choice (Graves 2016). In fact, Graves expressed a lot more anger toward the in-party split with Miller that he did toward his Democratic opponent that year, the latter of whom he called a "friend" and a "fine public servant."

Graves easily defeated Miller in the Republican primary, possibly due to much higher name recognition. Also, it was a time of economic growth, and Kansas was doing relatively well. The same was not true of the Graves' ally, Frahm. Brownback aggressively organized churches, homeschoolers, and others in the religious right to gain traction. He worked tirelessly, pulling off the upset. Graves would later say that his single biggest regret as governor was not preparing Frahm for the race against Brownback. Graves, like many dispensers of the conventional wisdom in Kansas at that time, did not see Brownback as a serious threat. Graves realized his mistake only after it was too late.

In the general election, Democrat Jill Docking opposed Brownback with similar politics as Frahm. Docking was a moderate Democrat, a businesswoman from Wichita who had married into a prominent, Democratic, Kansas political family. Like Frahm, Docking stressed consensus and holding the line on taxes. The Docking family name would also appear to give her an advantage in the election. Finally, like Frahm, Docking avoided hot-button social issues such as abortion rights and same-sex marriage. However, it was not to be. Brownback won, later being reelected, and serving in the Senate from 1997 until 2011. Also notable in '96 were Brownback supporters' signature bumper stickers, featuring the message: "I'm a Brownbacker."

Was he truly standing on principle this whole time? Noam Scheiber, writer for *The New Republic*, raised questions about this in a 2006 article. Scheiber quoted former Kansas for Life (KFL) President Tim Golba, who stated that when Brownback ran for Congress in 1994, "it quickly became clear that there was little to discuss. Brownback was not only unfamiliar with the antiabortion lexicon, he had a habit of dropping the hints used by politicians on the other side." Golba also remembered Brownback likening himself to Senator Kassebaum, a pro-choice moderate.

According to Scheiber's profile, Brownback came to embrace the pro-life stand during his 1994 run for Congress, very shortly before the primary. His primary opponent that year was a perennial single-issue, anti-abortion candidate named Bob Bennie. Brownback began to co-opt Bennie's language on the topic. This occurred at the same time that KFL was becoming much more sophisticated, transforming their approach from lobbying, to recruiting and endorsing candidates. Initially skeptical about Brownback's late conversion to their cause, KFL would enthusiastically embrace his Senate run just two years later. Scheiber also notes Brownback's religious journey. Raised a Methodist, Brownback first became an evangelical, then converted to Catholicism with a particularly strong interest in Opus Dei. Even then, he continued attending both Catholic and evangelical churches. Yet Scheiber could not help but note the political timeliness of Brownback's conversions, happening right as KFL was becoming a major force in state politics.

GOD'S SENATOR

Brownback continued onto his service in the Senate, keeping his promise to his base by emphasizing socially conservative positions such as opposition to abortion, resistance to liberal and even moderate judicial appointments, and opposition to same-sex marriage. He even came into conflict with a president from his own party: George W. Bush. Bush sought to appoint his personal attorney Harriet Miers to a vacancy on the U.S. Supreme Court. Brownback opposed. Brownback stressed that he had concerns about Miers' lack of experience as a federal judge. However, the conventional wisdom held that Brownback's real concern was that she would be too much of a moderate, not a vote to overturn *Roe v Wade*. As in so many controversies, Brownback emphasized that he was standing on principle.

In addition to the usual antiabortion and anti-same-sex-marriage themes, Brownback developed a particularly strong interest in foreign policy, notable because this is not typically the best way to prepare for reelection. Foreign policy does not offer as many opportunities to bring largesse home to the home district or state. It should also be noted that Kansas has a lot of military facilities, providing a number of opportunities, along with its dependence on agricultural subsidies. Nothing doing for Brownback, however.

As he became increasingly devout in his conservative Christianity, Brownback gravitated toward foreign policy committee assignments, where he could work on issues such as opposing genocide in Darfur, Sudan, as well as human rights abuses that were prevalent in the southern part of that country. Brownback was also passionate about raising awareness regarding human trafficking, and would sometimes cosponsor bills with Democrats, including the liberal Senator Ted Kennedy from Massachusetts. Most notably, Kennedy and Brownback, along with their staff, were hard at work on an immigration reform bill, which would include a path to citizenship, until it was derailed after the September 11, 2001, terrorist attack. The 9/11 incident made security, not a path to citizenship, the order of the day. Brownback even sponsored a measure with Senator Hillary Clinton, to open up space in the U.S. capitol for prayer after September 11. Brownback's priorities were all about expressing his faith, not his partisanship.

As a very conservative senator, there weren't a lot of opportunities for common ground with Democrats, but there were some, and he took them. Later, Brownback would even appear with Senator Barack Obama in California, at Saddleback Church. The pastor at Saddleback was Rick Warren, author of the popular Christian book *The Purpose-Driven Life*. Obama and Brownback were appearing together to raise awareness about the importance of getting tested for HIV. The pairing was appropriate. Two of the populations most likely to resist getting tested were evangelical Christians and African Americans. The Brownback-Obama appearance was a sort of dream team, designed to raise awareness about the importance, and the two senators got tested themselves. This was the emerging Sam Brownback. He was a man of conversion, of religious faith, always acting on principle. This Brownback tacked very conservative on social issues, but made some surprising alliances, when it came to other opportunities to advocate for his values.

A RUN FOR PRESIDENT

Brownback took the next step in 2007, putting his hat in the ring as a candidate for the Republican presidential nomination. As a senator from a prairie state, Brownback focused on the Iowa caucuses. Iowa does not quite border Kansas, but it is nearby, with many similar demographics. The Iowa caucuses are of course the traditional kickoff to the presidential campaign primary season. Brownback failed to gain as much traction as he had hoped. When Arkansas governor Mike Huckabee entered the race, he played for many of the same voters—evangelical Christians—that Brownback was counting upon.

In the end, Brownback withdrew before the caucuses themselves. However, he left a legacy. First of all, this was when he published *From Power to Purpose*. That autobiography supplies a good deal of the material for this chapter. Second, when Brownback would later leave the Senate to seek the governorship of Kansas, the conventional wisdom throughout his governorship would settle around the idea that the actions he was taking, were designed to position him for another run for presidency. The idea seems to be that as governor, Brownback would have an opportunity to create a legacy at the state level that would be more clearly attributable to his own actions, as opposed to his actions being washed out as one of 100 senators. Oftentimes, only Washington insiders and political junkies truly know who is responsible for what in the Senate. So much happens in committees, behind closed doors. At the state level, Brownback would have a proving ground to try new, conservative thinking, and take credit for that. The idea that Brownback was positioning himself for another presidential run would take hold, as observers struggle to find explanations for why he not only took the actions he did as Kansas governor, but also refused to back down or change course when things did not turn out as planned.

PREDECESSORS IN THE GOVERNOR'S OFFICE

Brownback sought the governorship in 2010. The governor up until that time had been Mark Parkinson, who had been elected as lieutenant governor. His predecessor, Kathleen Sebelius, was Kansas governor beginning in 2003. Sebelius was a Democrat, elected in the climate in which Kansas Republicans were often split between moderates and conservative. Sometimes, particularly at the state level, Democrats in Kansas, though outnumbered, would win when Republicans nominated a conservative perceived as hard right. Sebelius defeated a former Kansas Speaker of the House named Tim Shallenburger, who had said during the campaign that schools could do with 1, 2, or 3 percent less funding in order to avoid a tax increase. Sebelius suggested instead that an audit of Kansas state government would produce more efficiencies. She pulled off the win, and was also reelected in 2006.

As a popular Democratic governor in a very Republican state, Sebelius attracted national publicity, including once giving the Democratic response to President George W. Bush's State of the Union Address. Sebelius was even vetted as a possible vice presidential nominee to run on the ticket with Barack Obama in 2008. It did not hurt that Sebelius had come forward early in support of Obama over his primary opponents, including Hillary Clinton. In a personal interview with political scientist Bob Beatty, Sebelius (2016) said being vetted as a possible vice president was one of the most exhausting and extensive things she had ever experienced. In the end, she was not the vice presidential pick, but after Obama's election, he proposed that she be the Secretary of Health and Human Services. Sebelius' background as the state's insurance commissioner, and her interest in healthcare, seemed to position her well for this role. She was confirmed by the Senate, and presided over the rollout of the Affordable Care Act, which was never popular in Kansas.

As lieutenant governor, Parkinson took over the governorship upon Sebelius' resignation in 2009. He was a former Republican—in fact, he was the leader of the Kansas Republican Party, a moderate who sought to build bridges by traveling to every county in the state. He switched parties, aware of the Kansas Republicans' increasingly conservative shift, and became Sebelius' running mate for her second term.

As governor, Parkinson led the state through the beginning, and the worst years, of the Great Recession. The state was forced to make deep cuts. However, Parkinson led an effort to leverage federal aid, plus a temporary sales tax increase (later made permanent under the Brownback administration) in order to cushion the blow. Parkinson's goal was to protect K–12 funding as much as possible, even though it meant deeper cuts to higher education and other state services. His reasoning for this rested on the fact that the state of Kansas had been called into court numerous times over state funding. In a series of cases known as the *Montoy* decisions, the Kansas Supreme Court ruled that the state of Kansas was not fulfilling its constitutional obligation for adequate and equitable education funding. In the early 1990s, under the administration of another Democrat, one-term governor Joan Finney, the Kansas Legislature had passed a comprehensive new education funding formula which decreased the school districts' reliance on local property taxes and increased reliance on state tax revenues.

Parkinson sought to protect this funding formula as much as possible. In the end, the state weathered the Great Recession with cuts to social services and other programs, but the school funding formula remained relatively intact. Parkinson announced that he would not be running for a full term as governor. Reaction among the state's political class was swift. *Kansas City Star* editorialist Mike Hendricks was extremely disappointed with Parkinson's decision. Hendricks argued that Parkinson was essentially conceding the office to the Republicans, who were poised to nominate Brownback (Hendricks 2009).

Political science professor Joe Aistrup wrote that Brownback would be the likely nominee, and the likely the next governor, and predicted a sharp rightward turn (Aistrup 2010). The *Wichita Eagle* editorial staff noted a report by a new group, the Kansas Policy Institute (KPI). Based in Wichita, and associated with the Kochs, the KPI argued that the state was not figuring its budget correctly, and that so-called budget cuts were in fact just reductions to budget increases. The *Eagle* editorialists were sharply critical of the KPI Report, arguing that the authors did not look at factors such as a loss of federal revenues going to the state. The KPI would later become a major supporter of the Brownback administration's budget policies.

Parkinson was clearly a moderate. He had negotiated a compromise to permit the construction of the new coal-powered power plant in Western Kansas that would supply electricity to Colorado. Sebelius' administration had denied the permit, arguing that it would produce greenhouse gases. In the era of global warming, Sebelius' administration argued that they had the authority to deny the permit on these grounds. Kansas legislators, particularly those in Western Kansas, strongly disagreed. Parkinson brokered a compromise permitting one power plant instead of two, but also requiring renewable energy portfolios. Thus, Parkinson alienated the most liberal Democrats, but developed a reputation as a conciliator and a compromiser. Such was Brownback's immediate predecessor.

2010: WINNING THE GOVERNORSHIP

Brownback got into the governor's race in 2010 with one enormous asset—his statewide name recognition as a U.S. senator, in office since 1997. His Democratic opponent looked good on paper. State Senator Tom Holland started his political career in the Kansas House of Representatives, by "flipping" a district in Franklin and southern Douglas Counties that had formerly been held by Republicans. This ability to win in mixed political territory made things look good for Holland, who went on to be elected to the state senate, where he serves to this day. However, despite Holland's strong advantages on paper, he struggled mightily with fundraising. He was only able to win backing from the party and a few labor unions, and Brownback swamped him with both name recognition and fundraising.

Brownback did not propose a "glide path to zero" or get into any specifics about taxes while seeking the governorship in 2010. One well-versed observer that year was Kansas Judge Phil Journey, who had also served as a conservative Republican state senator from the Wichita area. He recalled the 2010 campaign:

> Well, you know we went to the debate—we always go to the debate at the state fair, and you know I remember his road map, and the things he intended to try to promote. You know he tried to stay away in some ways from social issues and show the voting public that he has other things to accomplish, like improving the schools—he had a reading program, third grade or something like that, and all those things he had to do required a legislative enactment, so some of them didn't come to fruition.
>
> He talked about taxes; he talked about reducing the size of government like all small government conservatives. He answered that with those broad principles, but I do not remember any specific proposals that were anything other than a broad platitude of desire. You know, candidates can't get into the weeds of specifics until they know the specifics of what they are attempting to modify. (Journey 2018)

Journey noted that Brownback campaigned on traditional conservative themes like self-reliance, traditional family, and small government. However, he was not specific about any plans. For all an observer knew, Brownback was proposing more modest tax cuts like the ones that had passed during the moderate Graves administration. Brownback kept it general. Hendricks and Aistrup were among the few commentators to predict the sharp rightward turn, including with regard to budgeting, that would likely occur under a Brownback administration. Most others did not see it coming.

Brownback was running on his name recognition, popular issues such as his proposed reading program, and general, conservative themes. Even in the first year of his administration, Brownback did not hint at a "glide path." Instead, that policy would emerge rather suddenly in 2012.

Finally, one other factor probably put the nail in the coffin for Democrats in 2010—President Obama. The irony cannot be emphasized strongly enough: former Kansas governor Kathleen Sebelius, who remained quite popular throughout her service in Kansas, was a key official in Obama's cabinet. She oversaw the rollout of the Affordable Care Act, which was disliked by Republicans, including those in Kansas. Yet despite the Sebelius connection, not to mention his own Kansas heritage (his mother was from Wichita),

Obama was quite unpopular in Kansas, never coming close to winning the state's electoral votes, which have gone Republican in every presidential election since 1964.

In the end, the governor's election was not even close; 2010 was a Republican wave election, and Brownback benefitted. He defeated his Democratic opponent, Tom Holland, by a decisive 62 percent to 32 percent. Brownback swamped the underfunded Holland, and the stage was set for one of the most aggressive, state-level experiments in supply-side economics ever attempted.

REFERENCES

Aistrup, Joseph A. 2010. "Moderates May Want to Savor Success." *Manhattan Mercury*, May 12.

Brooks, Kelton. 2015. "Rehabilitation, Victims Programs Could be Among Budget Cuts Facing Kansas Prisons." *Hutchinson News*, June 10.

Brownback, Sam. 2007. *From Power to Purpose: A Remarkable Journey of Faith and Compassion.* Nashville, TN: Thomas Nelson.

Camerini, Michael and Shari Robertson. 2010. *Mountains and Clouds*. Documentary Film. Epidarvos Project.

Goossen, Duane. 2016. "State Economy Can't Go on Like This." *Salina Journal*, October 3.

Graves, Bill. 2016. Interview with Michael Smith, September 23.

Hendricks, Mike. 2009. "It Didn't Take Long for Parkinson to Sell Out to GOP." *Kansas City Star*, May 6.

Journey, Phil. 2018. Interview with Michael Smith, July 3.

Karr, Jerry. 2018. Interview with Bob Grover and James Calvert, May 18.

Loomis, B. A. 1993. *Time, Politics, and Policies.* Lawrence, KS: University Press of Kansas.

Lowry, Bryan and Max Londberg. 2017. "Inside Kansas Prison Riot Where Inmates 'Tried to Burn the Place Down." *Kansas City Star*, September 6.

Paynter, Ben. 2004. "Jesus Is in the Big House." *The Pitch*, February 12.

Pierce, Neal R. and Jerry Hagstrom. 1983. *The Book of America.* New York: W. W. Norton.

Scheiber, Noam. 2006. "The Many Conversions of Sam Brownback: The Apostle." *New Republic*, December 17.

Scott, Laura. 1995. "Solid Changes to Ag Board." *Kansas City Star*, C6.

Sebelius, Kathleen. 2016. Interview with Bob Beatty, October 13.

Chapter 3

Laying the Foundation for the "Great Experiment"

CHAPTER OVERVIEW

The election of Sam Brownback was, in a sense, the culmination of a long series of changes in Kansas politics. Kansas was traditionally dominated by the Republican Party. During this period, Kansas Republicans were known for relatively centrist leadership. Democrats won occasional victories, but Kansas voters typically defaulted to voting Republican. However, it should also be noted that Kansas has always had its share of political prairie fires. From the battles of Bleeding Kansas to the Populist Movement, then becoming a center of the "New Right," Kansas has always had streaks of radical and reactionary politics that disrupted the (Republican) status quo. The most recent change was in the late 1980s, as Republican "rebels" emerged from suburban Johnson County. Later, the "rebels" would become a bona fide faction of the Republican Party, frequently challenging and sometimes defeating moderate Republican incumbents, both in party primaries and in legislative leadership. The 1991 "Summer of Mercy" (antiabortion protests) brought out new voters to support this emerging plurality, which by 2003 had transformed itself into a political party unto itself, leading one of this chapter's coauthors to label Kansas a "three-party state." Meanwhile, the political emergence of wealthy capitalists Charles and David Koch provided funding to Republicans both in and out of Kansas who were willing to shift to the right on economic issues, including taxes.

BLEEDING KANSAS, SOCKLESS JERRY AND SLEDGEHAMMERS

Strong, even violent opposition to the status quo is nothing new to Kansas. The state's battle over statehood was a major trigger for the Civil War.

(Pinsker 2018). A mural of John Brown, wild-eyed and bearded, adorns the rotunda of the Kansas State Capitol (Peirce and Hagstrom 1983). Brown was an abolitionist who, together with his supporters, killed several pro-slavery settlers in Kansas before moving onward and eventually being tried and hung for attempting to start a slave revolt in Harper's Ferry, Virginia (A&E 2014). Internal battles and deadly skirmishes with militias from neighboring, pro-slavery Missouri ensued over whether Kansas would enter the Union as free or slave. The Free State side eventually won, and Kansas became known as "Bleeding Kansas." These deadly skirmishes are seen by many historians as a major impetus for the Civil War (Pinsker 2018).

In the 1880s, another aggressive challenge to politics-as-usual emerged. The Populist movement was spearheaded by farmers and laborers who sought, initially, to break up railroads and other monopolies (Bicha 1967). It had local heroes elsewhere, including Nebraska's William Jennings Bryan, who was nominated three times by the Democratic Party for President (Peirce and Hagstrom 1983). In Kansas, the most flamboyant figure associated with Populism was "Sockless" Jerry Simpson, a theatrical congressman from the southern part of the state. Bicha argues that Simpson valued theatrics more than policy. While his policy stands were generally consistent and part of the larger Populist movement, his actual reputation was based on his personality. From his nickname (Simpson once said "I don't wear them" in reference to *silk* socks, but the nickname stuck and he embraced it) to his rhetoric, to his exaggerated biography, Simpson cultivated a personality as a rabble-rouser (Snow 1978). His theatrics included standing in the doorways of the U.S. Capitol while whittling, and speaking in folksy colloquialisms until issues of injustice to farmers were raised, in which case he transformed himself into being articulate, dark, and angry (ibid.).

The Populist movement would come to a head in 1893, when Populists and Republicans each elected different slates of candidates to the Kansas Legislature. The Republicans appeared to have won, but the Populists charged voter fraud (Zeff 2014). Two different slates of candidates arrived in Topeka prepared to be sworn into office. Led by Speaker George L. Douglas, the Republicans bashed their way into the House chamber with a sledgehammer. Governor Lorenzo D. Lewelling, of the People's (Populist) Party, called out the National Guard, instructing Col. J. W. F. Hughes to bring their Gatling gun. However, the Guard consisted primarily of Republicans, including Hughes, and they refused to obey. The Populists capitulated after 48 hours, ending the Legislative War of 1893 (ibid.).

Kansas also had its share of other political entertainment and drama, including John R. Brinkley, the unlicensed "Goat Gland Doctor" and entrepreneur of early radio, who sought the Governorship in 1930 (Kansas Historical Society 2003), and Governor Fred Hall, who got himself appointed to the Kansas Supreme Court with his famous "triple play" moves in 1956, inspiring a move to change the way the state selects judges (Kansas Historical Society 2018). Yet these and other characters were not pursuing an ideological message. In terms of resistance to Kansas' usual status quo of moderate Republicanism, three movements stand out: the Bleeding Kansas era, the Populist/People's Party revolt, and the rise of the "rebel" Republicans starting in the late 1980s. However, many of the state's most notable Republicans exemplify a different tradition: cautious embrace of change.

ALF LANDON AND NANCY LANDON KASSEBAUM: CAUTIOUS CONSERVATISM

Contrasted to these political firebrands, Kansas Republicans were typically the party of the status quo and incremental change. Governor Alfred M. "Alf" Landon exemplified this trend well. Landon was one of the only Republicans to win a governorship west of the Mississippi River in 1932 (Kansas Historical Society 2004). Yet this governor was no anti-New Deal reactionary. Landon favored a number of state-level policies intended to counter the Great Depression. The Kansas Historical Society notes that "he introduced programs to bring economic relief that included tax reductions, a moratorium on mortgage foreclosures, state supported local relief, and a series of emergency banking laws; all without increasing the state debt" (ibid.).

Considered a progressive at the time, Landon exemplified an alternative to FDR's New Deal so well that he won the GOP nomination for President in 1936. He was defeated decisively, even losing Kansas' electoral votes—rare for a Republican—and winning only Maine and Vermont. Even so, he remained popular in his home state. Landon lived a long life, racking up numerous awards and honors, even receiving a personal visit from President Reagan on his 100th birthday (ibid.).

Landon's daughter Nancy Landon Kassebaum (now Nancy Kassebaum Baker) shares many of her father's values and approaches to politics. Elected in 1978, Kassebaum took office as the only woman among 100 U.S. Senators. According to the History, Art, and Archives site of the U.S. House of Representatives, Kassebaum earned a reputation as a moderate who supported the broad outlines of Republican budget and defense programs but remained independent on social issues. For instance, she supported a woman's right to have an abortion. She also backed programs for international family planning, which again brought her into conflict with conservative Republicans. In 1992, she cofounded the Republican Majority Coalition, a group that sought to counter the rise of the religious right in the party. She resisted the feminist label, noting on one occasion that she thought of herself foremost as a "U.S. Senator, not a woman Senator" (U.S. House 2018).

The U.S. House history site, which also features biographies of Senators, also notes that Kassebaum "enraged fellow Republicans" when she supported a crime bill backed by President Clinton in 1994. She also sought a bipartisan deficit reduction plan in 1997. In 2018, the retired Kassebaum endorsed Democrat Laura Kelly for governor against the outspoken, anti-immigration Kris Kobach, who had won the GOP nomination by only a few hundred votes (Woodall 2018). Kassebaum had retired in 1996, the same year that Sam Brownback was elected to the U.S. Senate. However, her successor was in fact Senator Pat Roberts—Brownback won that year's special election to fill the balance of Senator Robert Dole's seat, when Dole resigned to seek Presidency.

I LIKE IKE: KANSAS' HIDDEN HAND PRESIDENT

While Landon and Kassebaum are key figures, no single Kansan better exemplifies the state's establishment Republicans than President Dwight Eisenhower of Abilene. In his "hidden hand presidency," Eisenhower deliberately cultivated a reputation for being at ease, for example, by playing golf and taking naps (Greenstein 1982). As Greenstein notes, Ike was deliberately plain-spoken in press conferences. In newsreels, he was often portrayed relaxing. Yet behind the scenes, he was an aggressive negotiator, heavily involved in the decisions made by his administration. He was also known for a fiery temper.

Eisenhower was strongly centrist. As a U.S. Army General, he hid his partisanship. Democrats even tried to recruit him as a Presidential candidate (Perlstein 2009). In 1952, Eisenhower was nominated for President in a deeply divided Republican National Convention. In order to do this, he had to defeat the more-conservative Senator Robert Taft of Ohio. The cosponsor of the anti-union Taft-Hartley Act, Taft favored a strongly isolationist foreign policy and a rollback of the New Deal, including Social Security and labor laws. Eisenhower's triumph was a victory for Republicans who favored essentially maintaining the new, post–New Deal status quo: an internationalist foreign policy, acceptance of the core programs of the New Deal, and caution about any further expansions of government beyond those already established. As Perlstein notes, the convention was raucous. Eisenhower's supporters pulled some last-minute moves to exclude southern delegates who would have favored Taft, arguing that the voting in southern states, where Republicans were badly outnumbered and voting was marred by segregation, did not meet the party's standard for seating delegates. Perlstein notes that the anger of Taft supporters was an early harbinger of the conservative drive to remake the Republican Party, which burst onto the national scene with the nomination of Barry Goldwater for President in 1964. The conservative drive to take over the Republican Party would be late in coming to Kansas—but when it came, its impact would be enormous.

Ike's hidden hand was particularly notable in his opposition to Senator Joseph "Tail Gunner Joe" McCarthy and his anti-communist crusades (Lovett 2016). Outwardly neutral, Ike was wary of the public backlash that would ensue if he were to openly take the side of those being attacked by McCarthy. Outside the public eye, however, Eisenhower aggressively sought to undermine McCarthy, particularly when McCarthy turned against the U.S. Army. According to Lovett, Eisenhower's actions were instrumental in McCarthy's eventual downfall.

Ike was the archetype of what it meant to be a Kansas Republican in the mid-twentieth century. Appearing outwardly to be the nation's easygoing father figure, he actually worked hard to maintain a centrist status quo. Ike exemplified "the Establishment." Unlike some politicians from the state's earlier times, Kansas Republicans were political pragmatists who understood the importance of agricultural subsidies, water policy, and Social Security to their constituents. They mastered the art of denouncing radicals on one side, reactionaries on the other, all the while working government to the benefit of constituency groups.

BOB DOLE: CONSERVATIVE RHETORIC, CENTRIST POLICIES

By the time Robert J. Dole began his political rise, changes were afoot among Republicans. Barry Goldwater captured the party's nomination in 1964, announcing at the Republican National Convention that "extremism, in the defense of liberty, is no vice. And let me remind you that moderation, in the pursuit of justice, is no virtue." Ronald Reagan mounted a strong challenge to Richard Nixon and others for the 1968 Presidential nomination. The New Right gained steam through the 1970s, galvanized by organized opposition to the 1973 *Roe v. Wade* U.S. Supreme Court ruling legalizing abortion, and the proposed Equal Rights Amendment (for women) to the U.S. Constitution. They also used emerging computer technology and grassroots organizing effectively (Crichlow 2011; Perlstein 2014).

In his public life, Dole compiled a long record as pragmatic, not a conservative iconoclast. While generally opposed to Democratic presidents, Dole also cosponsored a major expansion of the Food Stamps program with liberal South Dakota Senator George McGovern. Dole considered this one of his biggest accomplishments (Dole 2012). Years later, Dole would eulogize McGovern as a close personal friend as well as a respected political rival (ibid.).

Like Eisenhower, Dole became an entrenched part of the political establishment. In Washington, he rose to power with a combination of ruthlessness and political pragmatism. He led the Senate Republicans from 1985 to 1996—Majority Leader from 1985–1987 and again in 1995–1996, Minority Leader the rest of the time (ibid.). He was also the party's campaign chair in 1972, the year his friend McGovern was decisively defeated by Richard M. Nixon. The Watergate Scandal would come to light shortly afterward, and Dole, a staunch party man, would hold out quite a while in defense of Nixon (Perlstein 2008).

While Dole was a pragmatic party man in Washington, DC, sometimes making deals with Democrats, he was not afraid to appear outspokenly, ideologically conservative at home. This came to a head in the first national election after Watergate. In 1974, Dole nearly lost his seat to challenger Dr. Bill Roy, a Democrat who was "seen as above politics," according to *Kansas City Star* reporter Steve Kraske (2014). Tapping into his famously acerbic, even mean demeanor, Dole launched one of the first antiabortion campaigns in modern U.S. politics. Only one year after *Roe v. Wade* was decided. Dole not only accused Roy of favoring "abortion on demand," he also demanded to know how many abortions Roy, a doctor, had personally performed. Roy declined to give a number. Dole's campaign move mobilized conservative church congregations, whose cars were leafleted during services. In the end, it worked. Dole not only pulled off the tight victory but also helped to launch the modern era of antiabortion politics (ibid.).

Dole's confrontational demeanor was again on display when Gerald Ford nominated him to be vice president in 1976. In a debate with Walter Mondale, Dole famously said that all twentieth-century wars had been "Democrat wars," a move that made his signature harshness visible to a national audience (Biography.com Editors). Actor Dan Aykroyd would later contribute to Dole's national fame with a notable *Saturday Night Live* impersonation emphasizing Dole's meanness and his well-known war injury to his right arm. When Aykroyd moved on, actor Norm McDonald continued the tradition. In 2000, Dole himself appeared on the show with McDonald, telling him, "you're not doing an impersonation of me. You're doing an impersonation of Dan Aykroyd doing an impersonation of me" (NBC 2000). Dole loved political humor (Dole 2000), but even when he joined in the joke, a little of his signature meanness showed.

Dole's most famous piece of legislation was another expansion of Federal power—the passage of the Americans with Disabilities Act (ADA) in 1990. Known for his severe war injuries, long postwar recovery, and nearly immobile right arm, Dole was a longtime champion of disability rights. The ADA's passage was one of his signature legislative accomplishments (Robert J. Dole Institute of Politics 2018).

Like his collaboration with McGovern on Food Stamps, the ADA again puts Dole at odds with the strongest conservatives. Among its provisions, the law requires numerous new accessibility regulations on any entity receiving federal funding, if it is building new facilities or making major renovations to older ones. As such, it has been sharply criticized as regulatory overreach (Howard 2011).

Dole never hesitated to harshly attack Democrats in public. No one faced more of these attacks than President Bill Clinton. Dole was one of Clinton's most noted antagonists. While Dole expressed some initial support for a bipartisan healthcare reform bill, in the end he became sharply critical. As Minority Leader, Dole was pivotal in the defeat of President Bill and First Lady Hillary Clinton's signature health care proposals in 1994 (Clymer, Pear, and Toner 1994).

Dole won the GOP nomination in 1996, something of a mixed blessing in a year of economic recovery. President Clinton was widely expected to win reelection, and he did. Dole seemed out of his element as a presidential nominee—a very different sort of job than being a Senate leader. Dole appeared curmudgeonly against the fast-talking Clinton. The Biography.com editors wrote that Dole, "was often criticized for being his own worst enemy." The signature harshness may have energized a formidable base of Clinton-hating Republicans, but it was not destined for the White House.

Bob Dole's political career encapsulates a changing political landscape in Kansas. Dole was a consummate insider. As a power broker, his most famous pieces of legislation were an expansion of public welfare benefits cosponsored with a liberal Democrat, and a new list of federal regulations intended to advance the rights of marginalized Americans. These hardly fit the mold of an unyielding, small government conservative. Yet Dole knew how to be a conservative, and his mean demeanor probably helped. His "abortion on demand" attacks against Roy and his key role in defeating the Clintons' healthcare proposals both embodied his ability to tack conservative when the need arose. In the end, though, Dole was more of a party man than an ideologue. He used his leadership roles to advance legislation, including legislation beneficial to farmers and other Kansas constituents.

This was not the kind of conservatism being sought by the Republican "rebels" who began their rise to power during the governorship of Mike Hayden.

FERTILE GROUND FOR THE NEW RIGHT

Kansas' Republican Party had experienced significant shift in its ideological direction starting in the late 1980s. As chronicled by Burdett Loomis in his book, *Time, Politics, and Policy: A Legislative Year* (1993), the Kansas

Republican Party began to split into moderate and conservative factions. The conservative "rebels" hailed mostly from Johnson County, the wealthy county located in suburban Kansas City. Loomis notes that the Kansas Republican Party had long had a rural cast, which fits well with this state, known as it is for being the setting for the *Wizard of Oz*. However, the demographic reality in Kansas had been a shift toward this suburban majority, which had been happening for quite some time. Johnson County was the center of the shift. Composed of both middle-class and wealthy suburbs outside Kansas City, Missouri, Johnson County is sometimes referred to as "cupcake land." It was particularly known in the 1970s and 1980s for being the epitome of suburban American life (Peirce and Hagstrom).

Johnson County was also growing throughout the late twentieth and early twenty-first centuries, but the trends shifted (Beinart 1998). From the 1950s to the 1970s, Johnson County's growth was primarily due to people relocating from the central cities of Kansas City, Missouri, and Kansas City, Kansas, the latter being a small, satellite city of Kansas City, Missouri, analogous to East St. Louis, Illinois. This was the stereotypical "white flight," exacerbated by the heavily publicized troubles of the Kansas City, Missouri School District, including a teacher's strike in 1974 and two U.S. Supreme Court desegregation rulings in the 1990s. As Beinart notes, the growth patterns shifted in the 1990s. By then, most Johnson County growth came from people relocating from rural Kansas, rural areas in neighboring prairie states, or other metropolitan areas—people who had never lived in the nearby central cities in the first place. Johnson County also experienced a good deal of internal shifts, with the northeastern part of the county—as of 2018, mostly represented in the state legislature by Democrats—becoming more diverse. At the same time suburb-to-suburb flight took residents further out into the periphery of the county, colonizing small towns like DeSoto, Gardner, and Edgerton, which became exurbs.

In between older and newer, the suburb of Olathe experienced particularly explosive growth, expanding from one high school as recently as the late 1970s, to six today. Olathe is now one of the largest cities in the state. Back in the 1990s, the changes were already well underway. Beinart suggested that Olathe—new, suburban, predominantly white, Midwestern, and increasingly populated by people moving there from rural areas—was ground zero for the growth of the religious right, a claim also reiterated by author (and Johnson County native) Thomas Frank in his 2005 book *What's the Matter With Kansas*.

Frank's book deserves some mention. Reprising with some irony a title first used by Emporia journalist William Allen White, Frank's book was a diatribe against the Republican Party, shortly after George W. Bush was reelected. Frank, a socialist, was adamant in his assertion that Kansas had come to embody a place where laborers and farmers had been bamboozled by the Republican Party into voting against their own best interests. While Frank believed that the white working class would be best served by democratic socialist policies akin to those later espoused by presidential candidate Bernie Sanders, he saw suburban and rural whites voting instead for the GOP due to the party's conservative stands on social issues and appeals to conservative Christians, who in turn see their cultural values as being under attack by secularism.

Widely discussed among Kansas' chattering class, Frank's book became a *New York Times* bestseller. However, it was not without its critics. Most notable among these was political scientist Larry Bartels. Under the memorable, long title, Bartles wrote the rejoinder, "What's the Matter With *What's The Matter With Kansas*" (2006), Bartels rebutted Frank's claims. Citing data from political science studies, Bartels argued that white-working class voters tend to be socially liberal. They are drawn to the Republican Party by economic, not social issues—particularly their concern that social welfare programs are being abused by those who could work and provide for themselves if welfare was not available.

Bartels' rejoinder would foreshadow the return of the "welfare abuse" campaign theme by Donald Trump in 2016. Also used by Brownback and Kris Kobach, the issue of public welfare (and, many argue, the racial stereotyping associated with it) was also used, effectively, by Richard Nixon in 1968 and 1972, Ronald Reagan in 1980, and Bill Clinton, a Democrat, in 1992 and 1996 (Perlstein 2014). Bartels also noted that it was college-educated white voters, not the white working class, that were drawn to the "New Right." Given Bartels' conclusions, it should come as no surprise that in Kansas, the rise of the New Right began, not in struggling rural areas, but rather in relatively wealthy Johnson County.

Governor Mike Hayden and the Kansas Republican leaders were not prepared for the rise of the "rebel" Republicans. Elected in 1986, Hayden was known for a folksy demeanor, and the occasional gaffe. Hayden hailed from rural, Western Kansas, which is not the state's population center. Hayden was attentive to agricultural issues, and would later serve as secretary of the Kansas Department of Wildlife and Parks from 2002 to 2011, under both Republican and Democratic governors (Kansas Historical Society 2011).

In the late 1980s, most Kansas Republicans were still pro-choice, at least at the state level. At any rate, they usually avoided the abortion rights controversy altogether, just keeping it off the political agenda and focusing on other policies like taking care of farmers, for example, regarding water rights and the construction of roads in rural areas. However, most Kansans were not farmers. The growth of suburban areas such as Johnson County meant that Kansas was becoming an increasingly metropolitan state. Furthermore, the wealthy, predominantly white climate of suburban Johnson County was fertile ground for the religious right to take root. As such, Johnson County legislators became prominent in the "rebel" movement of the late 1980s.

The legislative rebels argued that the state's Republican Party was not keeping up with the change in the direction of the national Republican Party under the Reagan presidency. They were upset that Hayden and other Republicans rarely mentioned abortion. They did not just want to hold the line on taxes, as other Republicans did. They wanted to cut taxes. This was especially important to their constituents, who were wealthier than Kansans as a whole, and therefore paid more under the state's progressive income tax brackets. The rebels began to challenge the state's moderate Republican leadership. They ran candidates against moderate Republican legislative leaders, sometimes scoring victories, for example, splitting the House and Senate so that the conservatives would dominate in one chamber and moderates in the other, forcing compromises in which they were allowed to pick some key committee chairs, and making it more difficult to get the two houses to agree (Loomis).

THE SUMMER OF MERCY AND AFTERMATH

In 1991, Kansas' abortion laws were still relatively liberal. Wichita's George Tiller was one of the only doctors in the United States to perform late-term abortions. Tiller's practice, plus the state's changing politics, made Kansas the site of a political storm. That year, national antiabortion groups chose Wichita as a site for highly publicized, national protests. The protests drew thousands from within Kansas, and out of state as well. Under the assertive leadership of Mary Kay Culp, Kansans for Life capitalized on the changing political climate to register voters and organize through churches (Hancock 2018). Shrewdly, these political insurgents began targeting low-turnout, party primary elections. Their strategy met with success, as the newly energized, newly registered antiabortion voters became a powerful bloc of frequent voters (ibid.).

The momentum kept shifting after that. Conservatives scored a major victory when David Miller became the party chair. Miller later resigned the position to oppose a popular, sitting Republican governor in 1998 (Graves 2016). His primary challenge to Graves was unsuccessful, but the simple fact that a GOP chair would not only decline to support his party's incumbent governor, but would resign to oppose him, spoke volumes about the shift in the Kansas Republican Party. Tiller was shot and killed by an antiabortion activist in 2009, after having been shot earlier in both arms (Stumpe and Davey 2009). Culp immediately denounced the act and stated that the right-to-life movement does not condone violence.

THE KOCHS

Also occurring during this period was the political emergence of Charles and David Koch, the owners of Wichita's Koch Industries, who inherited the business from their father, Fred Koch. Fred, in turn, was a cofounder of the archconservative, anticommunist John Birch Society (Duignan 2011). David Koch sought the U.S. Vice Presidency on the Libertarian ticket in 1980. However, the Kochs later decided to cast their lot with the Republican Party. In subsequent years, they funded organizations such as Americans for Prosperity, the American Legislative Exchange Council (ALEC), The Cato Institute, and various political candidacies in hopes of shifting the party's and the nation's political direction to the right on economic issues (ibid.).

In Kansas, the Kochs are known for their strong support—and heavy investment—in the Kansas Chamber of Commerce (Zeff and Jeffries 2016). The Kochs were active in funding political activities and groups prior to the election of Governor Brownback; however, they would have far more notice (and, for some, notoriety) in the state during his governorship than they did beforehand. The political activities of the Kochs are also discussed in several of this book's other chapters. Charles Koch is a Kansan, residing in Wichita, while David lives in New York.

CONCLUSION

By 2003, the coauthor of this chapter had labeled Kansas a "three-party state," with moderate and conservative factions effectively functioning as separate parties who deeply distrusted one another, the Democrats rounding it out (Smith 2003). Democrats were able to exploit the GOP divisions, for example, with the election and reelection of Governor Kathleen Sebelius, who would later become U.S. Secretary of Health and Human Services in the Obama administration. Still, the conservative faction was ready to capture the party nomination and then win the big prize, once the right election-year climate came into being. A few years later, the Great Recession and Obama's unpopularity in Kansas would be just the ticket. The stage was being set for a Brownback governorship.

REFERENCES

Bartles, L. M. 2006. "What's the Matter with What's the Matter with Kansas?" *Quarterly Journal of Political Science,* 1, 201–226.

Beinart, P. 1998. "The Christian Right Moves to the Suburbs." *The New Republic,* October 18.

Bicha, K. D. 1967. "Jerry Simpson: Populist Without Principle." *The Journal of American History*, 54(2), September.

Biography.com Editors. 2018. "Bob Dole Biography." *Biography.com*, January 17. https://www.biography.com/people/bob-dole-9276436.

Clymer, A., R. Pear, and R. Toner. 1994. "The Healthcare Debate: What Went Wrong? How the Health Care Campaign Collapsed—A Special Report." *New York Times*, August 29.

Critchlow, D. T. 2011. *The Conservative Ascendancy: How the Republican Right Rose to Power in Modern America.* Lawrence, KS: University Press of Kansas.

Dole, B. 2012. "George McGovern, the Man Who Never Gave Up." *Washington Post,* October 21.

Duignan, Brian. 2011. "Charles and David Koch: Businessmen." *Encyclopedia Britannica.* https://www.britannica.com/biography/Charles-and-David-Koch.

Frank, T. 2004. *What's the Matter With Kansas? How Conservatives Won the Heart of America.* New York: Henry Holt.

Graves, Bill. 2016. Interview with Michael Smith, September 23.

Greenstein, F. I. 1982. *The Hidden-Hand Presidency: Eisenhower As Leader*. Baltimore, MA: Basic Books.

Hancock, P. 2018. "How Moderates Lost Control of the Kansas GOP, and Why They're Unlikely to Win It Back." *Lawrence Journal-World*, July 15.

History.com Editors. 2018. "John Brown's Raid on Harpers Ferry." *A & E Television Networks*, December 13. https://www.history.com/this-day-in-history/john-browns-raid-on-harpers-ferry.

Howard, P. K. 2011. *The Death of Common Sense: How Law Is Suffocating America.* New York: Random House.

Kansas Historical Society. 2017. "John Michael Hayden." *Kansapedia.* https://www.kshs.org/kansapedia/john-michael-hayden/17127.

Kansas Historical Society. 2003. "John R. Brinkley Papers." *Kansapedia.* https://www.kshs.org/kansapedia/john-r-brinkley/11988.

Kansas Historical Society. 2017. "Alfred M. Landon." *Kansapedia.* https://www.kshs.org/kansapedia/alfred-m-landon/12126.

Kraske, Steve. 2014. "Bill Roy Will be Remembered for Almost Defeating Bob Dole in 1974." *Kansas City Star*, June 3.

Loomis, B. A. 1993. *Time, Politics, and Policies.* Lawrence, KS: University Press of Kansas.

Lovett, C. C. 2016. "On the Side of the Angels and the Fall of Joe McCarthy." *Emporia State Research Studies,* 51(1), 8–29. http://academic.emporia.edu/esrs/vol51/lovett.pdf.

NBC. 2000. "Presidential Bash 2000." *Saturday Night Live.* Dir. Lorne Michaels. VHS.

Office of the Historian, United States House of Representatives. 2018. "Kassebaum, Nancy Landon." https://history.house.gov/People/Detail/16096.

Perlstein, Rick. 2008. *Nixonland: The Rise of a President and the Fracturing of America.* New York: Scribner.
Perlstein, R. 2009. *Before The Storm: Barry Goldwater and the Unmaking of the American Consensus.* New York: Nation Books.
Perlstein, R. 2014. *The Invisible Bridge: The Fall of Nixon and the Rise of Reagan.* New York: Simon & Schuster.
Pierce, Neal R. and Jerry Hagstrom. 1983. *The Book of America: Inside the 50 States Today.* New York: Warner Books.
Pinsker, Matthew. 2018. "Bleeding Kansas." *History.com.* https://css.history.com/topics/bleeding-kansas.
Robert J. Dole and Elizabeth Dole Archives and Special Collections. University of Kansas. n.d. "The Americans with Disabilities Act (ADA); Senator Dole as an Advocate for the Disabled." http://dolearchives.ku.edu/topics_ada.
Smith, M. A. 2003. "Kansas: The Three Party State." *Campaigns and Elections,* 1(21).
Snow, R. F. 1978. "American Characters: Sockless Jerry Simpson." *American Heritage,* 29(2).
Stumpe, J. and M. Davey. 2009. "Abortion Doctor Shot to Death in Kansas Church." *New York Times*, May 31.
Woodall, H. 2018. "GOP Stalwart Nancy Kassebaum Picks Democrat Laura Kelly over Kris Kobach." *Kansas City Star*, September 18.
Zeff, S. 2015. "If You Think It's Ugly Now in the Kansas Statehouse, You Should've Seen 1893." *KCUR,* June 4. http://www.kcur.org/post/if-you-think-its-ugly-now-kansas-statehouse-you-shouldve-seen-1893#stream/0.
Zeff, S. and A. Jefferies. 2016. "Election Question: How Are the Kochs Influencing Campaigns in Kansas This Year?" *KCUR*, October 20. http://www.kcur.org/post/elections-question-how-are-kochs-influencing-campaigns-kansas-year#stream/0.

Chapter 4

Supply-Side Economics in U.S. Politics

CHAPTER OVERVIEW

Supply-side economics gained prominent attention when it was proposed and implemented during the administration of President Ronald Reagan in the 1980s. A significant part of Sam Brownback's 2010 campaign for governor of Kansas was based on this economic philosophy; he proposed, and the Kansas Legislature passed supply-side concepts during his first term in office (2011–2014). This chapter explains some of the ideas, conjectures, and implications related to supply-side economics; moreover, examples of its application in the United States add perspective far beyond Kansas. This explanation relies mostly on the literature in economics, and it is intended to share some of this perspective in a nontechnical manner. No attempt is made to endorse these or other economic policies.

ORIGINS OF SUPPLY-SIDE ECONOMICS

Although supply-side economics applied to the U.S. government is a twentieth-century phenomenon, Bartlett (1981, 14) traced some vestiges of the intellectual roots to Ibn Khaldun, a fourteenth-century Muslim philosopher who argued in his work, *The Muqaddimah*, that high taxes were often a factor in the collapse of empires. In 1971, Jean David Boulakia published an article about Khaldun in the *Journal of Political Economy*. Bartlett noted that Robert Mundell was editor of that publication at the time and accepted Boulakia's article for publication. In addition, Bartlett states that the *Wall Street Journal* published a long passage from *The Muqaddimah* September 29, 1978, and Ronald Reagan mentioned Khaldun during a press conference in October 1981.

Although most of the American public became aware of what was to be called supply-side economics during the Reagan administration, the history of the concepts behind supply-side economics goes back to at least Jean-Baptiste Say (1767–1832). Say's Law, which J. B. Say called the Law of Markets, is commonly condensed to something like *supply creates its own demand*. Moreover, many of the economists around the time of Say advocated for laissez faire (i.e., the government keeps its *hands off*) economic policies. Individual liberty and private property, instead of government interference with economic activity, coincidentally were focal points for many economic thinkers around the time of J. B. Say. Part of this was a rebellion against the Mercantilist era that was part of European history in the fifteenth through the eighteenth centuries; however, the bulk of the Mercantilists' literature was in the seventeenth century and they typically favored policies discouraging imports and encouraging exports. They thought this would foster faster growth and greater wealth in a country.

Adam Smith, David Ricardo, and others suggested trade, especially based on comparative advantage in David Ricardo's terms, is likely to increase economic growth and prosperity for both trading partners. The coincidence of supply-side economics and laissez faire economics is undoubtedly appealing to modern-era advocates of supply-side economics.

SUPPLY-SIDE ECONOMICS IN THE UNITED STATES

Perhaps the most prominent proponent supply-side theorist in the modern era is Arthur Betz Laffer. He earned a bachelor's degree with a major in economics from Yale in 1963, and he earned an M.B.A. (1965) and Ph.D. in economics at Stanford University in 1972. He was a chief economist at the Office of Management and Budget from 1970 to 1972. Later he joined the faculty at the University of Chicago (1974–76) and then transitioned to the University of Southern California (1976–84) and then Pepperdine (1984–87). He was regarded to be one of the writers of the People's Initiative to Limit Property Taxation (Proposition 13) that amended the California Constitution in 1978. He was an economic advisor to President Ronald Regan and much later to Sam Brownback.

It is generally agreed that the theory that came to be known as supply-side economics was created and promoted by Robert A. Mundell and Arthur B. Laffer, who were two faculty members at the University of Chicago. The influence of Mundell and Laffer was described by Domitrovic (2014, 15):

> There would have been no supply-side revolution without these two; and it was they who encouraged and challenged others to join in the cause. It was

> specifically Mundell and Laffer who reeled in virtually all major advocates of supply-side economics in the 1970s, from Robert L. Bartley, Paul Craig Roberts, and Jude Wanniski at the Wall Street Journal to Jack Kemp in Congress and Ronald Reagan on the presidential ticket.

Indeed, Mundell and Laffer began the revolution, and Laffer has promoted the revolution into the twenty-first century. Laffer's research has been in international economic theory. He was among the first to develop a plan for a common currency in Europe, and he pioneered the theory of a monetary and fiscal policy mix. Among his many honors was the Nobel Prize for Economics in 1999. He is often considered the co-founder of supply-side economics. During the years 1972–1977, Laffer was a consultant to Secretary of the Treasury William Simon, Secretary of Defense Donald Rumsfeld, and Secretary of the Treasury George Shultz. He was a member of President Ronald Reagan's Economic Policy Advisory Board 1981–1989. He also advised Prime Minister Margaret Thatcher on fiscal policy in the United Kingdom during the 1980s. His years in the Reagan administration earned his reputation as the leading expert on supply-side economics.

THE LAFFER CURVE

Early in his career, Laffer created the "Laffer Curve" and used it in his teaching during the 1960s and 1970s. In an article in *The Public Interest,* Jude Wanniski (1978a), recalled a 1974 dinner at a Washington (DC) hotel with Laffer, Donald Rumsfeld, chief of staff for President Gerald Ford, and Richard Cheney, Rumsfeld's assistant. When the dinner discussion turned to President Gerald Ford's Whip Inflation Now (WIN) proposal for tax increases, Laffer grabbed his napkin to sketch the curve as an illustration of the relationship between tax rates and tax revenues. Wanniski named this graphic description of taxation the "Laffer Curve," and he frequently referred to the Laffer Curve in his book, *The Way the World Works.*

The white cloth napkin, now displayed at the National Museum of American History, is Arthur Laffer's early scribblings about supply-side economics; it is illustrated in the Appendix.

The Laffer Curve (figure 4.1) is a foundational theory for supply-side economics. It illustrates the relationship between tax rates and the total tax revenues that can be expected by a government. The rate ranges from 0 to 100 percent. The Laffer Curve shows that at a tax rate of 0 percent, the government would collect no tax revenue; likewise, it would collect no tax revenue at a tax rate of 100 percent because no one would be willing to work for a wage that went entirely to the government. The underlying

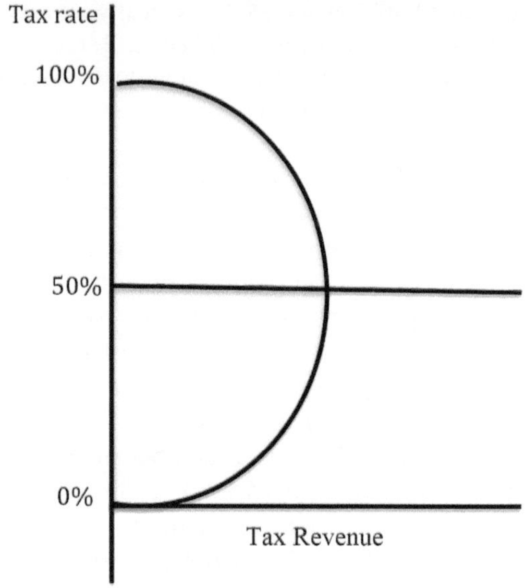

Figure 4.1 The Laffer Curve. *Source*: Author.

reasoning is that tax rates have both an arithmetic and an economic impact. If tax rates are lowered, the tax revenues will be lowered by the amount of the decrease in the rate, and the opposite is true when taxes are raised. For example, a one percent tax on $1000 collects $10, and a two percent tax would collect $20. The arithmetic suggests that doubling the tax rate doubles the revenue.

However, the economic impact recognizes the positive impact that lower tax rates have on work, production, and employment, and lower tax rates provide incentives to increase these activities. On the other hand, raising tax rates penalizes people; higher tax rates have the effect of diminishing incentive to work, to produce products, and to invest in such activities. The Laffer Curve shows that a tax increase may reduce business activity and raise less revenue than otherwise predicted, and a tax cut may increase activity and raise more revenue than might be predicted arithmetically.

Applied to a state, a relatively high sales tax rate, higher than neighboring states, would encourage consumers to cross state lines to do their shopping in order to avoid paying the higher taxes. Similarly, a high tax rate on state income taxes could encourage businesses to leave the state in order to realize a larger profit, and individual taxpayers might also leave the state or refuse to move to a state that has a high income tax rate.

The logic behind the Laffer Curve follows the notion of incentives. For example, if the tax rate on personal income is zero (i.e., no taxes exist on personal income), then the government would not collect any income tax revenue. (See point K on figure 4.2.) Similarly, if the tax rate is 100 percent, then the government would take all of the personal income (e. g., confiscate all personal income); few, if any, incentives remain for people to take the time or energy to earn personal income. Thus, the government would collect virtually no income tax revenue if the personal income tax rate is 100 percent. (See Point N on figure 4.2).

Laffer et al. (2008, 29) summarized the psychological motivation that underlies human behavior when dealing with high taxes:

> Why should workers or entrepreneurs break their backs if the government is going to take half or more of what they make? Moreover, higher taxes cause high-income earners to hire expensive accountants and lawyers to find tax shelters and other means to reduce their tax burden. And high rates can also induce people to move from high-tax places to low-tax places.

If tax rates are relatively low, the incentive for business owners and for consumers is much more favorable. Low income taxes may result in producing a business-friendly environment, attractive to business seeking a new home. Low property, income, and sales taxes are incentives for individuals to settle in a state, according to the supply-side theory. In Kansas, Governor Brownback's rationale for lowering income taxes, with the goal of eventually eliminating them, followed this line of reasoning. Governor Brownback described it as a "shot of adrenaline" to the economy, encouraging business growth and enticing businesses to move to Kansas.

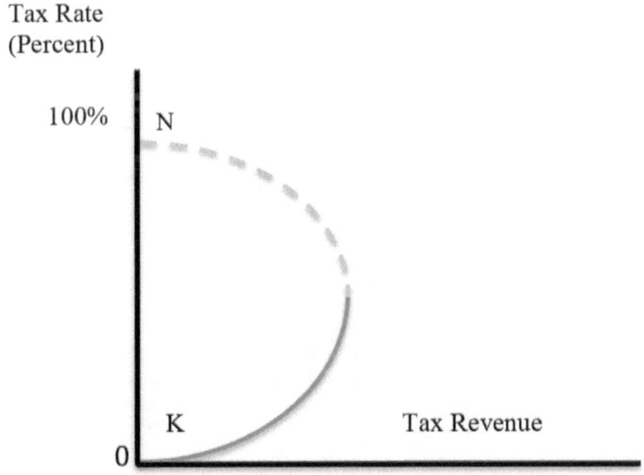

Figure 4.2 The Laffer Curve II. *Source*: Author.

Arthur Laffer's curve suggests that governments should follow these ideas when establishing tax policies:

1. When you tax something you get less of it and when you tax something less, you get more of it.
2. The best tax system helps make poor people rich, not rich people poor.
3. The higher the tax rate, the more damage to the economy and the greater the economic gain from reducing the tax rate.
4. If tax rates get too high, they may lead to a reduction in tax receipts, as demonstrated by the Laffer Curve.
5. An efficient tax system has a broad tax base and a low tax rate.
6. People, businesses, and capital move from high-tax to low-tax areas. (Laffer et al. 2008, 32–34)

Jude Wanniski, who was present when Laffer famously sketched his Curve on a napkin, propelled the Laffer Curve into mainstream thought when he prominently featured Laffer's theory in his 1978 book, *The Way the World Works*. A prominent writer for *The Wall Street Journal*, Wanniski devoted a section of his "Money and Tax Rates" chapter to the Laffer Curve and referred to it throughout his book. His explanation of Laffer's theory is represented in figure 4.3.

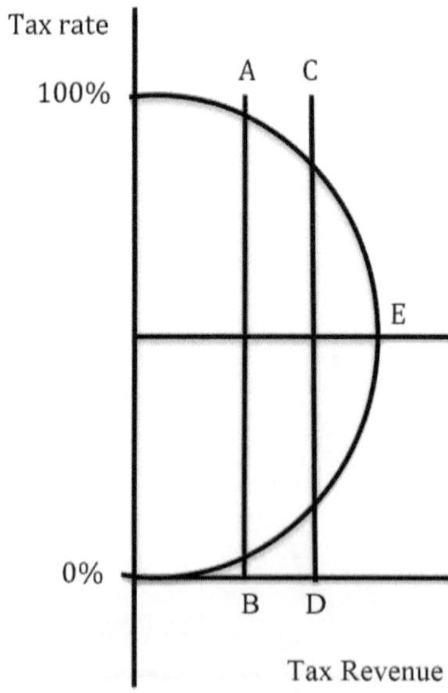

Figure 4.3 Wanniski Laffer Curve. *Source*: Author.

Wanniski acknowledged that if tax rates are at zero or 100 percent, no revenue is generated because at 100 percent taxation, no individual or business would have an incentive to work if all income went to the government. However, at point A, some segments of the economy might benefit with a small profit and be willing to work with a high tax rate. For example, during both World War I and World War II, taxes were extremely high, but businesses and individuals were willing to work to support the war effort. However, according to Wanniski, point A represents a very high tax with very low level of production, which is inconsistent with the actual levels of production in these times of war, and point B represents a very low tax rate and very high production.

Following Wanniski, by lowering a tax from point A to point C, revenue is expected to increase because of increased production; however, it is challenging to imagine the US economy expanding production very much during World War II, for example. A moderate increase in taxes from point B to point D in this model should would result in both increased production and increased tax revenue.

An important point to understand is that point E is not a specific number and as indicated earlier, it is not likely to be 50 percent, although it might be in certain circumstances. Instead, Point E is a variable number, which Wanniski describes as "the point at which the electorate desires to be taxed" (Wanniski 1978b, 98). At point E, if the government raises taxes, both output and revenue will go down. If, at point E, taxes are lowered, revenues will fall, even if production were to increase. The area above the horizontal line at point E represents Wanniski's prohibitive range for taxation because taxation is too high for encouraging production and tax revenue.

In summary, the Laffer Curve suggests that tax rates can enhance economic activity or discourage it by lowering or raising taxes. Whether a tax cut will raise or lower revenues depends upon several variables: (1) the tax system already in place when the new tax rate is implemented, (2) the time period, (3) tax loopholes available, and (4) what Laffer et al. (2008, 31) call "the ease of moving into underground activities."

When individuals and businesses are considering their "bottom line," they will make decisions that will put money into their pockets or the coffers of their business. Although a person may be willing to support government activity for the common good, many people will try to avoid paying more taxes than required by law.

An important point is that tax rates are not exact predictors of revenue to be gained; raising a tax by 50 percent would not necessarily increase revenue by 50 percent because that increase will have an impact that might diminish incentives for work, production, and investment that would result in less revenue than simple arithmetic might suggest. Similarly, the Laffer Curve suggests that lowering taxes could be an incentive for production and investment, and the result would be more tax revenue than predicted by simple arithmetic.

Before investigating application of the Laffer Curve in states, the next section will examine the U.S income tax system and results when income taxes have been cut.

U.S. INCOME TAX CUTS

The federal income tax was initiated in 1913 with a rate of seven percent on the highest income. It was increased during World War I to 77 percent for the top bracket. This high tax rate set the stage for a struggle on tax philosophy that continues today.

The United States has a graduated income tax; that is, the taxation rate increases according to the earnings of the individual or business. Important in a consideration of taxation is the "marginal" rate, which effectively the *extra* tax that must be paid on *extra* income. An important aspect of marginal tax rates is the generally accepted economic theory that the marginal tax rate can be so high that the individual may no longer have incentive to earn more or to invest more. A change in the tax rate on the individual's highest earnings can encourage or discourage a person to change the amount of work, if that is an option, as well as potentially changing financial instruments.

War Time Tax Increases

The income tax rate after World War I was substantially reduced during the 1920s. An influential person leading the effort to reduce taxes was Andrew W. Mellon, who was a successful banker and industrialist before serving as U. S. Secretary of the Treasury in the administrations of Warren G. Harding, Calvin Coolidge, and Herbert Hoover from 1921 to 1932. Mellon (1924, 12–13) summarized the country's tax dilemma following World War I:

> The existing tax system is an inheritance from the war. During that time the highest taxes ever levied by any country were borne uncomplainingly by the American people for the purpose of defraying the unusual and ever-increasing expenses incident to the successful conduct of a great war. Normal tax rates were increased, and a system of surtaxes was evolved in order to make the man of large income pay more proportionately than the smaller taxpayer. . . . For a short time the surtaxes yielded a large revenue. But since the close of the war people have come to look upon them as a business expense and have treated them accordingly by avoiding payment as much as possible.

Mellon believed that top earners would be willing to pay taxes if rates were 25 percent or lower, and he proposed tax cuts that Congress enacted during the 1920s. Between 1921 and 1929, the top marginal tax rate was reduced from 73 percent to 24 percent. Tax rates in lower income brackets also were cut substantially. An economic boom occurred around the same time.

Mellon (1924, 13) explained his philosophy based on his observations as a successful business executive:

> The history of taxation shows that taxes, which are inherently excessive, are not paid. The high rates inevitably put pressure upon the taxpayer to withdraw his capital from productive business and invest it in tax-exempt securities or to find other lawful methods of avoiding the realization of taxable income. The result is that the sources of taxation are drying up; wealth is failing to carry its share of the tax burden; and capital is being diverted into channels, which yield neither revenue to the Government nor profit to the people.

Therein rests the philosophy that serves as the foundation for the taxation stance of supply-side economics and the Laffer Curve.

The World War I scenario that resulted in tax increases to pay for the war repeated during World War II. Once again, tax rates were increased, and following the war, the incentive for paying the higher taxes no longer existed. Following World War II, the top marginal income tax rate was 91 per cent.

During World War II marginal tax rates were raised to 94 percent to fund the war effort and after the war ended, the top tax rate was reduced slightly to 85 percent, but Harry Truman in 1950 signed into law a tax increase to 92 percent and the top tax rate remained above 90 percent through the Eisenhower administration. By the end of the Eisenhower administration, the economy was lagging.

John F. Kennedy *Proposed* Tax Cuts

President John F. Kennedy took office in 1961 near the end of a relatively mild 10-month recession in the United States that ended in February 1961. However, the end of a recession cannot be recognized contemporaneously. President Kennedy encouraged legislation to cut the highest marginal tax rate from 91 percent to 70 percent, and he cut the capital gains tax on stocks and reduced lower income tax rates as well. Kennedy's tax policy was enacted in 1964, long after the recession of 1960–61 had ended.

Tax revenue increased from $48.7 billion in 1964 to $68.7 billion by 1968. Investment spending increased, economic growth surged, and national employment grew by more than 1 million jobs during these four years. Although it is obvious this followed implementation of the tax cuts, it important to remember that the economy was already expanding before the 1964 tax cuts. The unemployment rate fell to the lowest peacetime level in 30 years.

Surprisingly, the distribution of taxes paid indicated that the lower tax rates on the rich resulted in the rich paying a larger share of the tax burden. People earning more than $50,000 per year increased the amount of taxes paid by 40 percent, and their tax share rose from 12 percent of the total tax revenue in 1963 to nearly 15 percent in 1966. Those with income of $1 million and more increased their tax payments from $311 million in 1962 to $603 million in 1965 (Laffer et al. 2008, 58–59). The tax cuts proposed by President Kennedy coincided with a faster paced economy.

Reaganomics

The economy wavered during the 1970s, and the nation was in a recession during the 1980 presidential campaign. Ronald Reagan began implementing his economic plan immediately after taking office in 1981. Congressman Jack Kemp and Senator Bill Roth led the tax cut effort, and a tax cut bill was signed into law in August 1981. The Reagan plan was a three-year phased income tax cut—five percent in 1981, 10 percent in 1982, and 10 percent in 1983, with implementation of an index against inflation beginning in 1985.

The first two years of the plan saw continued economic stagnation until 1983, when the nation experienced economic growth of 5.1 percent in the first quarter, followed by five consecutive quarters of more than seven percent. By the end of 1984, six million more jobs had been created during Reagan's presidency, and that number grew to 17 million more jobs by the time Reagan left office in 1989 (Domitrovic 2014, 64).

Arthur Laffer, an influential member of the President's Economic Policy Advisory Board, was a strong proponent of the economic plan adopted by Congress in 1981 and stood firm when other leaders in the administration were skeptical that the plan was working when little progress was observed in 1982. The principles Laffer supported can be described as follows:

> Given a good marginal tax cut, people who earn more keep a greater share of their new earnings than they had before. This results in a race in the economy for new investment, new business creation, and new hiring. There is greater demand for money after a marginal tax cut, and it all serves the purposes of 'real' expansion in the economy, as opposed to fodder for inflation and tax hedges. (Domitrovic 2014, 65)

Arthur Laffer et al. (2008, 88) summarized the progress of the U.S. economy as a result of the supply-side policies implemented during the Reagan administration:

> The economy continued to grow throughout the decade at a 3.5 percent real rate and didn't slip into a recession until late 1990. The National Bureau of Economic Research in 1999 declared the period 1982–99 one continuous megaeconomic expansion, "the longest sustained period of prosperity in the twentieth century." Despite another very brief eight-month contraction in 2001, the economic spurt continued through 2007, though in 2008 it was teetering on the brink of recession.

Voodoo Economics

The concept of supply-side economics was controversial from the beginning of Reagan's presidency, and George H.W. Bush referred to it as "voodoo economics." Although the elder Bush campaigned as a Reaganite and uttered his promise, "Read my lips--no new taxes," he broke that pledge promise in 1990. Bush agreed to a tax increase with congressional leaders in an effort to reduce the budget deficit and balance the budget. This decision caused a rift within the Republican Party, causing some conservatives to display signs at the 1992 Republican Convention, "Read My Lips--No Second Term" (Laffer et al. 2008, 119).

In addition, raising taxes did not accomplish both of its intended goals, which were to boost the economy and reduce the federal budget deficit. Around the time President Bush agreed to higher taxes, the economy slid into a recession and federal spending increased. Instead of reducing the federal debt, the budget deficit, which was $149 million during President Reagan's last year in office, increased to $290 million in 1991. Spending increased by 20 percent during President Bush's four years as president, and tax revenues decreased despite the increase in the tax rate for the highest earners.

It is generally recognized that the tax increases under President George H.W. Bush contributed President Clinton's election in 1992. President Bush and Congress raised the top income tax rate from 28 to 30 percent. A few years later President Clinton raised the highest tax rate to 36 percent and added a 10 percent "millionaire surcharge." Even with this relatively high effective tax rate of 46 percent, it was substantially less than the 70 percent top marginal tax rate of 1980.

In 1994, the Republicans took control of Congress, and President Clinton worked with Republicans to implement a supply-side approach to promote free trade, cut the capital gains tax, and tighten the federal budget. During the Clinton administration, the stock market flourished, and the federal budget moved to a surplus. However, the stock market declined in 2000, causing a reduction in tax revenues and return to a budget deficit.

George W. Bush Tax Cuts

George W. Bush became president as the country slid into a recession, followed by the terrorist attacks of September 11, 2001. In January 2003, Arthur Laffer and Stephen Moore met with President Bush and a small group of economists in the White House. That meeting resulted in a bold application of supply-side strategies:

> We believe that the supply-side tax cut package President Bush agreed to in that meeting in the West Wing of the White House that morning helped airlift the economy out of the fire and helped assure his re-election less than two years later. (Laffer et al. 2008, 137)

The resulting plan initiated tax cuts intended to spur the stock market and encourage business spending. Passed by Congress in May 2003, this plan reduced the dividend tax from 39.6 to 15 percent, cut the capital gains tax from 20 to 15 percent, reduced the highest personal income tax rate from 39.6 to 35 percent, and lowered the tax on investments on plant machinery and equipment. Stocks climbed 20 percent in the two years following the tax cuts.

> President Bush's tax rate reductions made it less expensive for the job-creating class to expand their businesses, to raise the capital for new plants and equipment, and to hire new workers. And the result was the job market shook off its lull of the early 2000s. Between 2003 and the end of 2007 some 8 million jobs were created, or about 150,000 new jobs a month. . . . (Laffer et al. 2008, 142)

The tax cuts President Bush encouraged appear to be based on supply-side ideas. These include reduced tax rates for investors and businesses designed to increase economic growth, create more jobs, higher profits, and more revenue from taxes.

SUPPLY-SIDE ECONOMICS: MORE THAN TAX CUTS

Although tax rates are a fundamental part of supply-side economic theory, other economic variables are part of the bigger picture:

- Free trade
- Stable prices and sound money
- Light and efficient regulation of industry

- Reform of welfare policies to encourage work
- Generous immigration policy
- Less costly and more efficient government (Laffer et al. 2008, 36)

As this list suggests, supply-side economics embraces a multi-faceted approach to government and social policy. The underlying value system is one that supports and enhances business to promote a flourishing economy. The priority is the economy and all aspects of society that support it, and the needs of such other considerations as quality of life, social equality, minority rights, labor, and befitting "the common good" may be recognized, but these variables are secondary to supporting economic activity. In other words, supply-siders are looking at the world through the lens of business or corporate success; a flourishing economy will result in addressing needs of the poor and provide resolution to many of society's ills.

However, supply-side economics cannot be described adequately as "trickle down" economics. This view suggests that if the rich are provided with tax advantages, their wealth and its benefits will eventually "trickle down" to the poorer households in society. Arthur Laffer and other supply-side economists dismiss this criticism and point out that during the three decades of the implementation of supply-side theory, many people became very rich:

> In fact the vast, vast majority of the people who got rich over the last twenty-five years were not rich at the start of this period, and a good number of these people were lower middle class or poor. . . . Enterprising people in huge numbers took advantage of the opportunity to amass fortunes. That's the American way. (Laffer et al. 2008, 40)

Furthermore, Arthur Laffer insisted that the proportion of taxes paid by the rich has increased. As shown in table 4.1, the top 1 percent of earners in the U.S. in 1980 accounted for 8.5 percent of total income and increased to 21 percent in 2005. Although the increase in proportion grew for the top 5 percent, 10 percent, and 25 percent also, note that the total share of income

Table 4.1 Share of Income Earned

Earning Share (%)	*1980 (%)*	*2005 (%)*
Top 1	8.5	21.0
Top 5	21.0	33.0
Top 10	32.1	44.4
Top 25	56.7	66.1
Top 50	17.7	13.4

Source: Internal Revenue Service, Sept. 2006. Update (in Laffer et al. 2008, 40).

for the top 50 percent declined from 17.7 percent in 1980 to 13.4 percent in 2005. Laffer et al. point out that, indeed, the rich have been getting richer during this time period because of the supply-side economic policies implemented during the Reagan administration, and while the number of very rich increased, the people who became wealthy included many people in the lower and middle range of earners. According to supply-side economics proponents, the following scenario resulted:

> America cleared away the speed bumps on the path to prosperity and became an economic opportunity society. Enterprising people in huge numbers took advantage of the opportunities to amass fortunes. That's the American Way. (Laffer et al. 2008, 40)

During this same period of time, the tax rate for the top 1 percent declined from approximately 70 percent in 1980 to 35 percent in 2005, but the income tax share of the top 1 percent of earners increased from approximately 20 percent in 1980 to 40 percent in 2005 (Laffer et al. 2008, 41). The point here is that tax rates have decreased substantially during this period, but the amount of revenue generated has also increased substantially, supporting the premise that higher tax rates do not necessarily increase revenue.

STATES AS LABORATORIES

The Tenth Amendment of the U.S. Bill of Rights declares that all powers not granted to the federal government by the Constitution are delegated to the states. Consequently, states have the authority to establish economic policies and regulations to address their unique circumstances, and states can be case studies for the policies that they have adopted and the results they have achieved.

One of the earliest applications of supply-side economics was in California. After World War II, California's population was soaring, the demand for housing was strong, and home construction was booming. At the same time, California government was growing in order to provide services, and inflation was a national phenomenon. Property values increase dramatically and this led to higher property taxes, which placed an increasing burden on many in California. This was especially challenging for Californians on fixed incomes and a taxpayer revolt occurred in 1978. Responding to taxpayers' upset with their property tax bills, the California legislature passed a constitutional amendment that was ratified by a statewide referendum called Proposition 13, which capped property taxes at their 1975 value and limited annual increases to the rate of inflation.

Inspired by California's Proposition 13, the Massachusetts legislature also passed a series of laws and ballot initiatives during the years 1979 to 1982 that reduced property taxes, capital gains tax rates, and excise taxes in addition to capping spending. According to Brookes (1982), the result was a decline in the unemployment rate, an upturn in personal income, and a substantial increase in state revenue. The results were so astounding that this period of time and economic growth became known as "the Massachusetts Miracle."

Brookes (1982, 194) compared the California tax burden to that of Massachusetts:

> If California had a right to be furious over their taxes, the people of Massachusetts had far more right. Whereas property taxes in California had reached an average of about 2.8 percent of market value, in Massachusetts they had reached nearly 4.5 percent, or 61 percent above even the California level before the passage of Proposition 13. Whereas property taxes had been providing about 28 percent of total California revenues, they were now raising almost 46 percent of total revenues in Massachusetts, the highest proportion in the nation.

The high property taxes became a major issue in the 1978 Massachusetts governor's race, and Michael Dukakis, the incumbent governor, was defeated soundly in the Democratic primary. In that race, Democrat Edward J. King took a position based on the California Proposition 13 movement and proposed lower property taxes. Brookes' analysis of the voting patterns showed that Dukakis' vote count was an inverse relationship to the property tax rate in counties statewide; when tax rates were high; his vote total was low compared with his opponent, and vice versa. Brookes suggested that a person could have predicted King's margin of victory in a town by the relative size of its property tax.

Similarly, an economic analysis at this time by Robert Genetski, of Harris (Bank) Research Department suggested that a state's pattern for economic growth was related to that state's tax burden. According to Genetski, " . . . those states displaying above-average increases in their tax burden tending to show below-average economic growth and vice versa" (Brookes 1982, 195). This conclusion was supported by Genetski's report that of 37 states with lower-than-average growth in their tax burden, all but three had above-average economic growth. Similarly, of the 14 states with high tax rate growth, all but three had below average economic growth. In this study, Massachusetts had the ninth-fastest growth in tax burden and had the third-lowest growth in income and economy (Brookes 1982, 195). By contrast, Florida ranked 38th in tax burden growth but had the fourth fastest growing personal income.

Edward King was elected governor of Massachusetts in 1978 and began to implement his campaign promise to lower taxes with the cooperation of the legislature, which in 1979 lowered the capital gains tax by 60 percent over three years. King also promoted a cap on increased local government spending and encouraged local governments to decrease property taxes; more than half of the cities and towns complied by lowering property taxes. By mid-1980, Massachusetts was outperforming the nation in personal income growth and job growth, while lessening the tax burden (Brookes 1982).

Brookes (1982, 202) summarized his economic principles, using the Massachusetts example, and it illustrates a supply-side perspective:

> It is no longer possible to pursue economic policies that punish productive human capital through taxation, regulation, and bureaucracy. Either it will stop producing or (as in the case of Massachusetts) it will go elsewhere. The only real limits on the future growth of the Massachusetts economy now lie in the state's ability to attract professional people to come into the state to live—an ability that seems strong if the state continues to ease the taxing burden it places on individuals.

Brookes also foresaw the transition of the nation's economy from manufacturing to a largely technological economy based on ideas. He cited the contributions to the economy of the state's public and private higher education institutions, including Harvard, MIT, Boston College, Boston University, and University of Massachusetts, to provide the intellectual capital to grow the technological economy in a state with limited natural raw resources.

> The state that launched the American Revolution by throwing tea in Boston Harbor to protest taxes is once more demonstrating that the most important ingredient in the generation of real economic wealth is still the freedom of the individual human mind to express and develop its ideas. (Brookes 1982, 202)

The Wall Street Journal recognized the Massachusetts change in tax policy, and an article by James Ring Adams described the Massachusetts turnaround and linked it to the Laffer Curve theory that suggests high tax rates can cause economic stagnation. The article brought national attention to Arthur Laffer and to the concept of supply-side economics.

Laffer et al. (2014) conducted an economic study of the fifty states to address the question: "Do state and local government economic policies redistribute income, or do they redistribute people?" (xvi) Their study examined the impact of various kinds of taxes on public services and the state's economy. For example, their study of the 11 states that introduced an income tax over the past 50-plus years compared with the remaining 39 states revealed the following points:

- Each of the states implementing an income tax lost tax revenues relative to the other 39 states.
- Those 11 states implementing an income tax had their gross state product shrink in comparison with the other 39.

- Tax burdens rose in the states implementing an income tax.
- Each state's economy underperformed in comparison with the other 39. (Laffer et al. 2014, 15)

Among the studies of states and the economic income of taxes, Laffer et al. (2014) compared the nine states with the lowest tax burden as a share of personal income with the nine states with the highest tax burden as a share of personal income. The main points results are summarized below.

- The nine lowest tax burden states have more full-time equivalent education employees.
- The nine lowest tax burden states are increasing the number of full-time equivalent education employees faster.
- The nine lowest tax burden states pay the education employees less per FTE.
- For non-welfare public service employees, the lowest tax burden states provide more workers, are increasing their numbers faster, and are paying them less.
- The highest tax burden states hire more welfare employees, pay them more and are growing at nearly the same rate as the nine lowest tax burden states. (76)

Laffer et al. (2014) summarize this comparison of the highest and lowest tax burden states:

> It's hard to imagine a greater contrast—low taxes, high growth, plentiful public services, and less welfare versus high taxes, anemic growth, insufficient public services, and lots of public welfare workers. (76)

Laffer and his associates have conducted studies of all fifty states to determine the impact of various kinds of taxes on such factors as economic growth, public services, education, state population growth, state business growth. Their studies indicate that no- and low-tax states like Texas, Arizona, New Hampshire, and Florida are finding that they are experiencing population growth and their economies are flourishing, and their climate is not the determining factor. Their research findings suggest that tax structure does make a difference in a state's economy and quality of life:

> Such has been the experience of modern-day tax reformers, folks like us who have studied and analyzed tax codes state by state and have solid data to demonstrate beyond a reasonable doubt that Americans are in fact moving at high rates away from high income tax states and into low and no income tax states. This is not a hypothesis, not an idea, not some abstract conclusion. It is a data-driven fact. (Laffer et al. 2014, 105)

With a background of more than 40 years as an advocate for low taxes, Arthur Laffer had become a big name in conservative political circles, and Kansas Governor Sam Brownback was aware of Laffer's work. In 2011, following his election as Kansas governor, Brownback hired Arthur Laffer as a consultant to devise a plan that would turn around the Kansas economy.

ANALYSIS: APPLYING SUPPLY-SIDE ECONOMIC THEORY

The Marginal Tax Rate Explained

Before exploring the application of Laffer's theory to tax cuts generally and to Kansas in particular, it is important to note that the marginal tax rate is virtually always greater than the average tax rate with a progressive income tax. A simple example might help. Imagine two children standing together on a large scale at a veterinarian's clinic. Their total weight registers as 100 pounds; obviously, the average weight is 50 pounds. Now, if a teenager steps onto the scale at the same time, the total weight increases to 210 pounds and the average weight increases to 70 pounds. The marginal, which is the extra weight from an extra person, is 110 pounds because the change in the total weight was 110 pounds divided by the change in the number of people, which was one additional person. The marginal of 110 cannot be smaller than the average of 70.

Although the diagrams that Arthur Laffer drew were simplified (i.e., the marginal and average tax rates were implicitly the same), the idea is that when the government has especially high marginal income tax rates, the incentive to earn income (typically from wages and salaries at work) is less. In other words, when tax rates become so large that workers start to believe that it is not worth it to work as much, then tax revenues may fall.

Impact of Tax Policy

A couple of points are crucial in evaluating the impact of tax policy. Some workers have little control over their amount of work. Some are required to work a set work schedule and risk their employment being terminated if they endeavor to scale back in terms of hours of work. These workers face an "all or nothing" dichotomy. We might expect that these workers are less sensitive to tax rate changes than workers who have some control over the amount they may work.

Some workers control the amount of work they perform. Let us go through an example where workers must decide if they wish to work an extra hour.

Let us use a wage rate of $100 per hour, for example. (This worker's gross pay before taxes would be approximately $200,000 per year working 40 hours per week times 50 weeks.) Let us further assume no other taxes exist on wage income for simplicity and clarity of exposition. If the worker were to face a marginal tax rate of 70 percent, then the worker would take home an extra $30 and the government would collect an extra $70 in personal income tax revenue from the extra hour of work. Remember, we are simplifying with no other deductions from the worker's pay. As long as the marginal tax rate is less than 100 percent, the worker should have some extra income after tax income when the worker earns an extra $100.

Part of the reason the Laffer Curve and supply-side economics in general is so controversial is because the impact on income tax revenues of this economic theory depends on income earners' reactions to change in the tax rate. Moreover, their response(s) may not be symmetrical. If highly productive and high-income workers are already working long hours, then a cut in their marginal tax rate should produce two potentially competing incentives. First, the lower marginal tax rate should increase the opportunity cost of non-work time (e.g., leisure); this worker has the incentive to work more because leisure is now relatively more expensive. For example, the $100/hour worker may sacrifice $100 in gross pay to watch a television show for an hour and an extra $30 in take-home pay. At the same time, the worker has an effective increase in income when evaluating after-tax income.

Relatively larger changes in the marginal tax rate can produce dramatic changes in after tax income, especially when considered over a year. Will the worker still wish to work long hours each day without much non-work time (e.g., time for personal hygiene, relaxation, and sleep) if the worker is able to adjust? Let us explore what happens to this income effect when the marginal tax rate falls from 70 percent (as it was for the federal personal income tax when President Reagan took office) to 50 percent in the first round of Reagan-era tax cuts that were implemented at the federal level. Our hypothetical worker would have something less than a $30,000 increase in after tax income. The actual amount would depend on the hours of work along with the actual structure of tax rates. However, the key question is will the worker likely work more or less? Certainly, the opportunity cost of that television show increases; however, will the worker scale back with all of these extra funds?

The Laffer Curve suggests the worker will work more when marginal tax rates are reduced in the upper-part (the dashed-segment illustrated in figure 4.4) of the Laffer Curve. Furthermore, the empirical evidence was clouded by recessions in the early 1980s.

Instead of a federal government budget closer to balance, it was farther away by the end of the decade of the 1980s. When President Reagan took office, the national debt was approximately an accumulated $1 trillion. By

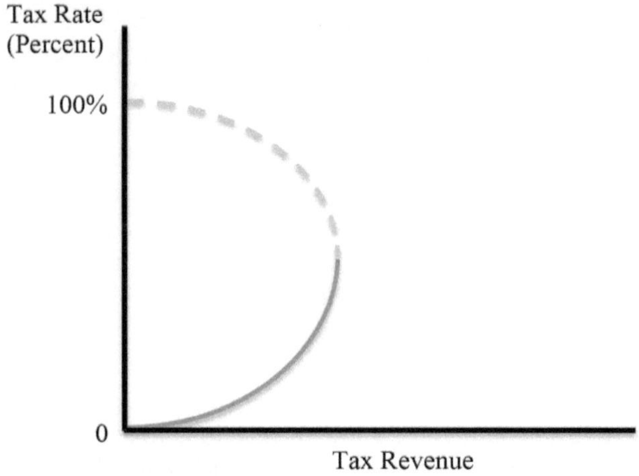

Figure 4.4 The Laffer Curve III. *Source*: Author.

the time he left office eight years later is was nearly $3 trillion. Once again, several things happened simultaneously, and it seems inappropriate to suggest that supply-side economics is fully responsible for this outcome.

Applying the Laffer Curve in Kansas

The points that are germane in Sam Brownback's grand experiment with supply-side driven tax cuts for the Kansas Economy relate to income tax rates in the Kansas economy before the grand experiment. Based on calculations from the Emporia State University Center for Community Research, the highest marginal tax rate of 6.45 percent for Kansas personal income remained in the lower echelons of a Laffer-style curve when Sam Brownback was elected as governor in 2010.

Moreover, in 2013, the highest marginal tax rate for Kansas adjusted personal income was 4.9 percent. In 2014, the rate was 4.8 percent. In 2015 and 2016, it was 4.6 percent. The reduction from 6.45 percent to 4.6 percent was a 28.68 percent reduction in the highest marginal tax on adjusted personal income.

Although it depends on the circumstances, generally speaking, tax cuts (i.e., specifically lower marginal tax rates) potentially could generate more economic activity, which can be translated into economic growth. Sometimes it is challenging to isolate the impact of tax cuts because other policies or events may be changing at the same time as tax rates. Moreover, economic conditions can have an impact on changing tax policy.

From a public finance perspective, changing tax rates is likely to have an impact on the aggregate tax revenue collected by a governmental entity; however, the amount of tax revenue is not a linear function of tax rates, which is a part of what the Laffer Curve is intended to illustrate.

Beyond the non-linear structure of the Laffer Curve, the illustrated symmetry raises an interesting issue, especially related to the Kansas personal income tax structure. Recall that all of these Kansas (marginal) personal income tax rates in the era of Governor Brownback were less than 5 percent. Furthermore, it should be recognized that mathematically average tax rates cannot exceed marginal tax rates; therefore, both marginal and average Kansas personal tax rates were less than 5 percent in this era.

This is important because it would take a highly convoluted Laffer Curve to increase Kansas personal income tax collections with reductions in tax rates. A few caveats are important to explore here.

The implied structure of the Laffer Curve is based on a national model, where the migration of firms and organizations is more challenging than just moving across the state line, for example in the Kansas City metropolitan area.

Apply the Curve with Caution

Is the Laffer Curve symmetrical? In other words, must a 50 percent tax rate generate the most tax revenue? Although the answer is almost certainly to be "No," the slope of the curve is a key. Moreover, the complexity of the issues surrounding state-level public finance means it is necessary to explore beyond what happens when rates are lowered in the bottom segment of the Laffer Curve.

Kansas personal income taxes do not exist in isolation. The federal personal income tax and taxes related to Social Security, Medicare, and the like are likely to be paid by those paying Kansas income taxes. Moreover, the migration of people and organizations would have some impact. In technical terms, these would shift the Laffer Curve rather than move along it.

Although these migrations were implicitly part of Governor Brownback's experiment, some additional considerations may have been overlooked. For example, sometimes, the individual gain in disposable personal income from a tax cut, especially among those with relatively large tax liabilities, may influence a taxpayer to take advantage of rather large changes in disposable income (i.e., income after taxes or what is commonly called take-home pay). In fact, these high-income earners are likely to be able to scale back and still have an increase in disposable income up to a point.

Growth matters and part of the allure of tax cuts is the prospect for faster economic growth; however, that growth sometimes does not meet expectations. The following excerpt is from a *New York Times* interview that addresses that issue:

> N. Gregory Mankiw, a Harvard University economist who was chairman of the President's Council of Economic Advisers under the younger Mr. Bush, said tax cut supporters exaggerate the possible growth benefits while opponents overemphasize the budgetary cost. "A reasonable rule of thumb, in my judgment, is that

about one-third of the cost of tax cuts is recouped via faster economic growth," he said. (Baker 2017)

The impact of tax cuts in Kansas is explored more thoroughly in chapters 8 and 9.

CHAPTER SUMMARY

The conceptual basis for supply-side economics can be traced to a fourteenth century Muslim philosopher, but it is generally agreed that the theory that came to be known as supply-side economics was created and promoted by Robert A. Mundell and Arthur B. Laffer. The foundational theory of supply-side economics is succinctly characterized by the Laffer Curve, which illustrates that tax rates can enhance economic activity or discourage it by lowering or raising tax rates. The theory was most notably implemented during the presidency of Ronald Reagan and again by President George W. Bush. Supply-side-related ideas have been tried in Massachusetts and California. Arthur Laffer and the Laffer Center have conducted research on the impact of taxes and state policy on the economy and social services in a state. After his election as governor of Kansas, Sam Brownback called upon Laffer to help him craft a plan to employ a "great experiment" to transform Kansas.

REFERENCES

Baker, Peter. 2017. "Arthur Laffer's Theory on Tax Cuts Comes to Life Once More." *The New York Times*, April 25. https://www.nytimes.com/2017/04/25/us/politics/white-house-economic-policy-arthur-laffer.html.

Bartlett, Bruce R. 1981. *Reaganomics: Supply Side Economics in Action.* Westport, CN: Arlington House.

Brookes, Warren T. 1982. *The Economy in Mind.* New York: Universe Books.

Domitrovic, Brian. 2014. *The Pillars of Reaganomics.* San Francisco: Laffer Center at the Pacific Research Institute.

Laffer, Arthur B. 2014. "Time Wounds All Heels, July 22, 1994." In *The Pillars of Reaganomics,* edited by Brian Domitrovic, 121–129. San Francisco: Laffer Center at the Pacific Research Institute.

Laffer, Arthur B., Stephen Moore, and Peter J. Tanous. 2008. *The End of Prosperity; How Higher Taxes Will Doom the Economy—If We Let It Happen.* New York: Threshold Editions.

Laffer, Arthur B. Dr., Stephen Moore, Rex A. Sinquefield, and Travis H. Brown. 2014. *An Inquiry into the Nature and Causes of the Wealth of States: How Taxes, Energy, and Worker Freedom Change Everything*. Hoboken, NJ: Wiley.

Mellon, Andrew W. 1924. *Taxation, the People's Business*. New York: Macmillan.

Wanniski, Jude. 1978a. "Taxes, Revenues, and the 'Laffer Curve.'" *The Public Interest*, Winter 1978.

Wanniski, Jude. 1978b. *The Way the World Works: How Economies Fail—And Succeed*. New York: Basic Books.

Chapter 5

Implementing the Experiment

CHAPTER OVERVIEW

Sam Brownback's election as governor signaled the end of moderate leadership and a swing to a much more conservative agenda, which Brownback outlined in his campaign. During the first two years of his administration, Brownback introduced a number of social and economic programs that would significantly change the state; included was a radical tax reform plan.

Years three and four of Brownback's first term saw the passage of additional legislation to support his social agenda and to continue the "glide path to zero" income taxes. In this chapter we describe the legislation supported by Governor Brownback and the Republican-dominated legislature during his first—legislation and policies that became issues in the 2014 election.

LAUNCHING THE EXPERIMENT

Brownback had campaigned for the governorship on general, conservative themes like low taxes and traditional family values. He won decisively, as did Republican candidates for the Legislature. The GOP now commanded a 92-33 seat majority in the house, thanks to the pickup of 16 seats in the 2010 Republican wave. The senate was not on the ballot that year, but a party switch by one member increased the Republican lead to 32-8 (Schremmer 2011).

Commentators expected a shift to the right, but they lacked specifics. Early signaling by the new governor gave little indication of what was to come. True to form, he did rule out tax increases, calling instead for the elimination of wasteful programs (Klepper 2011a). However, one of Brownback's first stands seemed to moderate this—the new governor actually opposed a tax cut. Legislators were clamoring to roll back a recent 1 percent sales tax increase, passed during the Parkinson administration to cope with the Great Recession revenue shortfalls. Brownback opposed the rollback, saying, "We're short of resources for the state, and I don't think it's something that we should be doing at this time." He added, "Our fiscal situation is not stable" (Klepper 2011a). Noting that schools were facing cuts, Brownback also suggested they be given increased flexibility with their reserves (Milburn 2011).

Brownback's priorities seemed to be on something else besides taxes. As during his campaigns and his service in the U.S. Senate, the new governor stressed his opposition to abortion, as well as promising to promote marriage by removing disincentives from welfare policies (Carpenter 2011a). One reporter predicted that Brownback would focus the vast majority of his attention on social issues, not the budget, writing,

> The wish list includes abortion, adult entertainment, evolution, the smoking ban, adoption, faith-based initiatives, "covenant" marriage, DUI and seat belt laws, sex education, gambling, divorce, and concealed weapons. Family values, defined variably by politicians, will be touted by legislators seizing the moment (Carpenter 2011b).

Brownback did turn to the budget in his inaugural State of the State Address. He proposed to eliminate eight state agencies and 2,000 state jobs that were currently unfilled. He argued he could reduce the coming year's budget by $750 million while increasing K–12 funding and protecting higher education and social services. He also proposed Rural Opportunity Zones featuring temporary tax-free status for new residents, other targeted tax breaks, early childhood education centers in low-income school districts funded by tobacco settlement money, and a review of Medicaid lead by Lieutenant. Governor Colyer, a doctor (Klepper 2011b).

The new governor's first budget proposal put forth the details. While he did propose additional state funding for K–12 education, it was not enough to offset the loss of federal stimulus money, resulting in a net cut. He also proposed a spending freeze until June 30, spinning off the Kansas Arts Council into a nonprofit, and eliminating state funds for public broadcasting. The other agency eliminations involved consolidating freestanding boards and agencies into other governmental entities, rather than simply zeroing out their funding. This included the merging of the Kansas Parole Board into the Department of Corrections (ibid.). He also proposed a $10.2 million cut in mental health services (Carpenter 2011c). In addition, he sought a $200 million transfer of highway funds to the general funds (Editors 2011a). He created an Office of the Repealer to identify and propose elimination of unneeded regulations, arguing that this would bring job growth (Carpenter 2011d).

Results of the 2011 session included two new abortion restrictions, eliminating most late term abortions and requiring parental consent for minors (Carpenter 2011e). In other news, the speed limit on some rural interstates was raised to 75 mph (Editors 2011b).

Regarding executive power, Brownback consolidated hiring in the Department of Administration, removing agencies' authority to hire their own employees and raising alarm by commentators (Loomis 2011). In the end, the FY 2012 budget passed only after protracted negotiations between the House and Senate. It made cuts to K–12 funding and social services, some quite deep, but did not eliminate the Arts Commission (Carpenter 2011f).

While Brownback did advocate and win major budget cuts that year, his focus was not on cutting taxes. Instead, the governor was attempting to close a budget shortfall and compensate for dwindling federal stimulus money. The tax cuts he proposed were highly targeted, and some even included offsetting increases, or "pay fors" (Klepper 2011c).

The year 2012 opened with Brownback headed to Iowa to campaign for Texas governor Rick Perry, whose presidential bid was endorsed by Brownback a few months earlier (Associated Press 2012a). In addition, Wichita got some bad news as Boeing announced the closure of its Wichita plant (Associated Press 2012b). Lt. Governor Colyer's study group released their proposal for Medicaid reform. They proposed contracting with for-profit managed care providers. Advocates for those receiving services raised concerns about their well-being (Editors 2012a). Brownback also proposed eliminating the cap on the ability of school districts to self-fund through higher property taxes, known locally as the Local Option Budget. Eliminating the LOB cap would widen the funding gap between wealthy and poor districts. In addition, his proposal would remove the weighting of school funding, which had provided additional monies for at-risk students (Marso 2012). Finally, the governor offered a tax-cut proposal, but featuring more "pay-fors" than what would eventually pass the legislature. The details of this proposal and the final legislation are discussed later in this book.

As if that was not enough to do, the Legislature also had redistricting on the agenda that year. Kansas uses no nonpartisan or bipartisan commissions to draw maps after the decennial census, leaving that power entirely in the hands of the Legislature. Legislators could not agree on a map, and that protracted process may have further worn down their energies (Smith 2012).

With a Legislature confronted by Brownback's proposals for sweeping change, plus a protracted and failed redistricting process, the stage was set for the surprising moves that launched the Kansas Great Experiment.

SUMMARY OF THE 2012 TAX PACKAGE

During the 2012 legislative session, the legislature passed, and the governor signed, one of the most extensive (and most controversial) tax cutting plans in the nation. In summary, the legislation:

- Slashed state income taxes by roughly $3.7 billion over five years;
- Projected budget deficits reaching $2.5 billion in 2018;
- Collapsed the state's three-bracket system to two brackets starting in 2013;
- Cut the highest income tax rates to 4.9 percent from 6.45 percent and 6.25 percent;
- Reduced the lowest tax rate to 3 percent from 3.5 percent,
- Allowed the state sales tax to drop by six-tenths of a cent in 2013;
- Retained deductions for charitable contributions and interest on home mortgages—deductions Brownback wanted eliminated;
- Eliminated tax credits for food sales tax rebates and credits for taxpayers who have to work and must care for children, disabled dependents or spouses; and
- Exempted non-wage business income for an estimated 190,000 (later revised to 330,000) limited-liability companies (LLCs), sole proprietorships and the like.

The non-wage business income exemption was intended to create jobs. Brownback hoped that business owners would use the dollars saved to energize the economy; he viewed the tax package as an opportunity for the state to remake its business climate while providing needed state services: "We're going to move this forward and make it work and take care of our fundamental services," Brownback was quoted in *The Kansas City Star* (2012a). In that same interview, Brownback promised to fund core services like schools and roads, but vowed he would continue to cut state government. "We're going to keep pruning state government any place that we can," the governor said.

Passage of the tax bill included some drama and gamesmanship. When the tax plan was proposed, Brownback had proposed a number of ways to cover lost revenue, but lawmakers received a cool reception from constituents who didn't want to give up their home mortgage interest deduction. In response, conservative legislators in the House developed their own plan that would lower taxes without eliminating many tax deductions and credits. Eventually, a divided Legislature passed a bill that lowered taxes but did not eliminate the popular deductions for home mortgage interest and charitable contributions.

The Senate effectively had killed the tax revision bill in March. Soon after its defeat, some senators reversed themselves and passed the bill to resume negotiations. When the Senate seemed to falter at more modest tax cuts, the

House went ahead and passed the more radical tax cut bill, which was signed into law by the governor.

The process was raucous. The initial Senate bill contained multiple "pay fors:" the elimination of income tax credits and deductions for poor workers, charitable contributions, and interest on home mortgages (Hanna 2012). These were stripped from the bill by the more conservative House. The bill failed in the Senate on a 20-20 vote. Brownback spoke to several Republican senators about their votes (ibid.). Two hours later, the Senate passed the bill 29-11 after adding still another budget-buster—a cut in the sales tax rate from 6.3 to 5.7 percent (ibid.).

The nine senators who switched sides told reporters that they did this to further the process, apparently a reference to getting the bill into a conference committee. One switcher, Majority Leader Steve Morris, told a reporter that he did it to keep the process moving (ibid.). Another switcher, Dick Kelsey, said "most of the Republicans flipped out of respect for the governor." A third, Senator Les Donovan, gave the clearest indication that the purpose of the vote was to get the bill into negotiations when he said, "Are we going to get everything the governor wanted? Probably not . . . . It's going to be hard to put something together that works for everybody" (ibid.).

What happened next was summarized by reporter Tim Carpenter: "In an unexpected move, the House abandoned its own version of tax reform and voted 64-59 to embrace the Senate bill" (Carpenter 2012). This move undermined the Senate's intention of getting the bill into conference committee and sent the bill, stripped of pay-fors, straight to the governor's desk. He signed it in short order, leaving many of the nine senators who switched sides feeling betrayed.

IMPACT OF THE TAX PLAN ON STATE REVENUE

The question whether the tax plan would succeed or fail and its impact on critical state services were a concern to many Kansans, who believed that the governor's approach would decimate state services. Forecasts showed that the tax plan would result in huge state deficits and have a negative impact on public education, public health, infrastructure, and other state services to the public.

The 2013 Legislature faced the specter of a huge revenue decrease. Governor Brownback acknowledged this challenge as the legislative session approached. While not offering a specific set of solutions, he noted the expected "hard dip" in revenue. At a December 2012 forum in Overland Park, Kansas, he recalled that he originally had proposed paying for the income tax cuts by retaining part of a penny sales tax scheduled to expire July 1, 2013, as well as eliminating several tax deductions, including deductions for interest on home mortgages and for charitable contributions.

Because those "pay-fors" did not pass the Legislature, Brownback urged the Legislature to consider again these ideas because of the impending $705 million decrease in revenue resulting from the 2012 tax cuts. As Cooper (2012a) reported in *The Kansas City Star,* "I think we ought to do some of the pay-fors that I proposed last year," Brownback said. Although he intended to cut some state services, Brownback vowed to support funding for education, public safety and medical services for the poor.

It was generally acknowledged that the governor knew when he signed the tax cuts into law that the cuts would leave a hole in the state budget, at least in the short term. Legislative fiscal analysts had predicted the tax cuts would cost the state about $3.7 billion in revenue over five years; however, Brownback and other advocates of the tax plan expected a short-term dip in revenue that would be replaced with tax revenue generated by economic growth resulting from the tax cuts—supply-side economics in action.

2012 ELECTION STRENGTHENS THE CONSERVATIVE MAJORITY

As the 2012 legislative session concluded, the 2012 election cycle began, and Brownback took the unusual step of endorsing Republicans running against other Republicans in the primary election (Editors 2012b). He made the decision at the last minute, making the announcement on July 13, less than a month before the election. Targets included Majority Leader Steve Morris and several moderate committee chairs.

Although Brownback had gotten the senate to approve his tax cuts in an unusual series of maneuvers, senate moderates not only groused about this, but also blocked some of Brownback's other priorities. Senators refused to go along with the governor's plan to change appellate court judge selection, rewrite labor laws to favor businesses, rewrite the school base funding formula, and link teacher pay to student achievement (Cooper 2012b).

Brownback was late to the party; the conservative challengers were already being backed by donors who receive financial support from the Kochs—the Kansas Chamber of Commerce and Americans for Prosperity (ibid.). Former governor Bill Graves attempted a last-minute effort to stump for the moderates (ibid.), but it was too little, too late. In the end, of twelve moderates targeted, nine were defeated, including Morris, shifting the balance of power sharply to the right (Smith 2016).

Democrats were unable to reverse these conservative gains in the general election. From 2012 to 2016, the new conservative majority would pass a good deal more of Brownback's agenda, including the appellate court change he sought, and a replacement of the school funding formula with block grants.

Following the 2012 elections, which increased the conservative stronghold in both houses of the Kansas Legislature, Brownback appeared ready to implement his small government/low tax agenda. The stakes for Kansas and Brownback were high, as stated in *The Kansas City Star* (2012c):

> His unapologetically bold agenda, backed with mounting political power, makes Kansas a proving ground for a range of conservative theory. If it works—kick-starting a particular prosperity in Kansas—the governor becomes a national rival to Christie and the rest. If it bombs, then Brownback's political career dead-ends in Topeka.

Indeed, the national spotlight was on Brownback and his "great experiment." Brownback had left his U.S. Senate seat to build a reputation as a conservative leader, and his travels suggested that he envisioned another presidential run:

> The Kansan with the soft-spoken charm and an aw-shucks demeanor has methodically built a resume that could energize any presidential prospects he might cultivate for 2016 or beyond even as, critics insist, he puts the state at risk. In recent months, Brownback has traveled the country touting the power of small government, low taxes and his efforts leading the state out of a budget hole and into a surplus. (Cooper Ibid.)

Despite, or perhaps because of, his legislative victories of 2012 by cutting taxes and privatizing Medicaid, the editorial board of *The Kansas City Star* (2012b) issued an ominous warning: "The hasty passage of the income tax cuts and the hurried start of KanCare are likely to haunt the state for a long time to come."

The stage was set for the 2013 legislative session, and Sam Brownback laid out his agenda in his address to the Kansas Legislature and his constituents.

GOVERNOR'S STATE OF THE STATE ADDRESS: KANSAS IS A SPECIAL PLACE

Governor Brownback, in his 2013 State of the State speech (Brownback 2013), listed five major areas to bring about legislative action: (1) conserving water, (2) fighting childhood poverty, (3) creating jobs and economic growth, (4) developing a two-year budget, and (5) instituting governmental reforms.

Although his speech did not reveal what he meant by "governmental reforms," the governor's staff had warned agencies to prepare for budget reductions that could amount to ten percent.

The State of the State speech, declaring Kansas as a "special place," set a tone for his vision for Kansas leadership in the nation—featuring smaller government and lower taxes:

> And as has been our tradition since before statehood, our place, Kansas, will not be timid in doing what is right, even if much of the Nation takes another way. Where others choose to raise taxes, we will lower them so our people have more money, not the government. Where other governments expand, we grow smaller. Where others choose to grow spending, Kansas grows jobs.

Brownback linked economic development to the tax structure. He said he would lobby legislators to sustain the 6.3 percent sales tax, which was scheduled to drop to 5.7 percent that June. He revealed that he would recommend that the upper state income tax rate of 4.9 percent be dropped to 3.5 percent and the lower income tax rate from 3.5 percent to 1.9 percent:

He stated that he did not favor government assistance programs: "We will help families economically, educationally, and socially. It will involve local efforts of intensive support, mentoring and pushing people to the job market, not another government program."

Brownback also challenged the authority of the Kansas courts to dictate school finance. His rationale:

> In the democratic system of checks and balances crafted by our Founding Fathers, the power to authorize spending public money was given exclusively to you, the Legislative branch. This is a core principle. The "power of the purse" is the primary power of the Legislature, not the Executive or the Judiciary.

He said that a ruling from the Shawnee County District Court on inadequate funding of schools would be appealed, and that the method of selecting members of the Kansas Court of Appeals and Kansas Supreme Court should be amended. He suggested that the "federal system" of appointing judges should be instituted—judges should be appointed by the governor and confirmed by the Kansas Senate. He said that he would support a law enabling the election of appellate judges and Supreme Court justices. The existing system in Kansas required a governor to select a nominee from among three finalists chosen by a committee composed primarily of lawyers.

In terms of reshaping state government, Brownback said lawmakers should merge the quasi-state controlled Kansas Turnpike Authority into the Kansas Department of Transportation, which is the province of the governor.

The conclusion of the 2013 State of the State address showed the intent of the governor to make Kansas an example for the nation: "Kansas is the heart of America. Let's make our place a shining example for the Nation to follow."

The governor's speech saw a positive position for the state economically, and his tax plan was at the center of his efforts to boost the state economy. Streamlining government and challenging the state's Supreme Court's authority over school funding were also large items on his agenda. Now let's examine the legislative session and how his vision was addressed.

This address and the direction of Kansas government was gathering attention nationwide. Noting that the 2012 election resulted in conservative Republicans taking over the Kansas Legislature to support the governor's small government and low taxes direction, *The New York Times* (Eligon 2013) acknowledged Brownback's so-called experiment had implications for other states:

> On Wednesday, lawmakers received a bill to inch the state closer to eliminating income taxes, a centerpiece of a broad legislative vision that many in the Republican Party here hope will serve as a model of conservative governance for other states, if not the nation, to follow.

The mood in the legislature was positive because the governor and majority of both houses were in agreement with the governor's plan; in fact, many were elected to support the governor. For the first time in many decades, Kansas government was dominated by conservative Republicans eager to transform government to their philosophy. What follows is a review of those bills indicative of that conservative philosophy.

MAJOR ISSUES DURING THE 2013 LEGISLATIVE SESSION

Among the major bills passed by the Kansas Legislature during 2013 were articulated in the governor's State of the State address, and a number reflected the conservative political philosophy of the governor and legislature. Included was a state budget that cut into state services and continued revision of the tax structure. In addition, such "hot button" issues as abortion, gun legislation, religious freedom, and school funding were passed by the legislature and signed by Governor Brownback.

Abortion

Abortion was a favorite issue of Brownback and many of his supporters. Bills were introduced to curb abortion by erecting roadblocks that would make it more difficult to get an abortion. House Bill 2253, which banned abortions based on gender, barred abortion providers from distributing sexual education materials to public schools, blocked all direct or indirect tax incentives for the procedure, and revised the state's informed consent materials given to those considering an abortion. The law also defined human life as beginning "at fertilization," and the law established a requirement to provide controversial information about a link between abortion and breast cancer. Abortion was a favorite issue with the Brownback administration; every year brought bills that challenged Roe vs. Wade, the federal law legalizing abortion in the United States.

On a related topic, the legislature passed legislation that reflects the condemnation of fetal cell use in stem cell research. Senate Bill 199 established the Midwest Stem Cell Therapy Center at the University of Kansas Medical Center. This bill states that all funds and facilities of the Center must be dedicated to treatments and research with adult, cord blood and related stem cells and non-embryonic stem cells and specifically prohibits the use of funds or Center facilities involving embryonic or fetal tissue cells.

Corporate Freedom from Government Intervention

Brownback's agenda included a strong pro-business stance, and several bills passed the legislature that weakened regulations and enhanced the position of employers while weakening benefits for workers. Kansas is a "right to work" state, which means that unions cannot require employees to join a union while working for an employer.

Corporate farming scored well during this legislative session. Senate Bill 168 amended law relating to the protection of farmland and agricultural activities from certain "nuisance actions." This law might be dubbed "The Corporate Farm Protection Act," essentially protecting corporate farms from litigation for such nuisance accusations that corporate farms pollute the water, air, or soil or otherwise impose a negative impact on the environment.

House Bill 2069 prohibits cities, counties, and local governments from requiring private employers to provide leave or leave compensation or to pay wages at a higher rate than the state or federal minimum wage. In general, the tenor of the legislature during the Brownback administration was anti-labor, and this bill is evidence of the pro-business attitude.

A further restriction on employees was Senate Substitute for House Bill 2022, which revises the Professional Negotiations Act and the Public Employer-Employee Relations Act by restricting the partisan or political purposes of professional employees' organizations (PEOs) and public employee organizations. The bill prohibits PEOs from using money deducted from members' paychecks for partisan or political activities, and PEOs are not allowed to require political contributions as a condition of membership.

Government Reform

In his State of the State address preceding this legislative session, Governor Brownback placed a high priority on government reform with few specifics; however, he stated his concern about the authority of the judiciary and Appointment of Court of Appeals Judges was revised (House Bill 2019) to enable the governor, with the consent of the senate, to fill any vacancy on the Kansas Court of Appeals. The governor must make an appointment within 60 days of receiving notice of a vacancy; otherwise, the Chief Justice of the Kansas Supreme Court, with the consent of the Senate, will appoint a person for the position. This legislation was a result of the governor's plea to challenge court authority over school funding, and addressing the Court of Appeals judges was a step toward additional legislation that would provide the governor a greater say in the appointment of Supreme Court justices.

The Senate passed a constitutional amendment (SCR 1601) that would permit the governor to appoint Supreme Court justices, with the consent of the Senate; however, the amendment died in the House.

Another governmental reform was related to the administration of assistance program for the needy and unemployed. Drug screening for Cash Assistance Programs (Senate Bill 149) authorized the screening of applicants or recipients of cash assistance and Unemployment Insurance (UI) benefits for unlawful use of controlled substances. If the results of screening are positive, the person must complete a substance abuse treatment program and a job skills program. A person who fails or refuses to complete either program is ineligible for UI benefits. This new law addressed the governor's concern that people should be working and contributing to the economy—not takers of government programs. The bill included additional provisions for subsequent test failure and added members of the Legislature to the list of state employees who are eligible for drug screening if a reasonable suspicion is present.

Governmental reform was extended to the retirement system for public employees, and retirees receive some benefit from these changes. HB 2213 modifies the Kansas Public Employees Retirement System (KPERS), the Retirement System for Judges (Judges), and the Kansas Police and Firemen's (KP&F) Retirement System. Among other things, the bill:

- Clarifies a vested member who terminates with 10 years of service without withdrawing the employee's contributions and interest may retire under early retirement provisions at age 55;
- Corrects internal references to ensure members retiring under either early retirement or normal retirement are eligible for the $4,000 retiree death benefit;

- Raises the cap on maximum KP&F member retirement benefits from 80.0 percent to
  90 percent of final average salary;
- Increases the KP&F employee contribution rate from 7.0 percent to 7.15 percent for all years of service to self-fund the benefit increase from the active KP&F employees; and
- Allows retired members of KP&F and the Judges plans who divorce after retirement to have the district court order the cancellation of the joint annuitant option for the ex-spouse.

The governor's strong religious convictions are evidenced in passage of the Kansas Preservation of Religious Freedom Act (House Bill 2203), which provides that government shall not substantially burden a person's civil right to exercise religion. The bill allows a person whose exercise of religion has been burdened or is substantially likely to be burdened to assert the violation as a claim or defense in a judicial proceeding.

This act is a subtle attack on gay rights. Although it has not been tested in the courts, the intent of the Preservation of Religious Freedom Act is to allow privately owned businesses to claim it is their religious freedom to refuse services or goods to individual or groups in support of activities in opposition to religious beliefs. For example, business owners who fervently believe that homosexuality is forbidden by their religion may refuse to provide good or services for such events as gay weddings or other activities intended for gays. It can also be used as a rationale for refusing to provide support for contraceptive services or means to employees or to organizations like Planned Parenthood.

Gun Legislation

Protecting Second Amendment rights to own and carry guns was a common theme during the Brownback administration. The Second Amendment Protection Act (Senate Bill 102) excluded from federal regulation any firearm, firearm accessory, or ammunition manufactured and owned in Kansas. The bill prevents any federal agent, state employee, or local authority from enforcing any federal regulation governing firearms if the firearms remain in Kansas.

Senate Substitute for House Bill 2052 amended the Personal and Family Protection Act (PFPA) to allow the possession of firearms on certain governmental property, including state and municipal buildings and requires adequate security measures at public entrances of state and municipal buildings in order to prohibit the carrying of any weapon into these buildings. School districts and the State Capitol were exempted although the law allows a licensee to carry a concealed handgun in the State Capitol. The bill authorized four-year exemptions for universities and other governing bodies to develop a security plan. The bill permits school districts, public and private post-secondary educational institutions, public medical care facilities, public adult care homes, community mental health centers, and indigent health care clinics to allow a licensed employee to concealed carry of a handgun if certain requirements are met.

The bill allows corrections facilities, jails, and law enforcement agencies to prohibit the carrying of handguns or firearms into the secured areas, and the chief judge of each judicial district may prohibit the carrying of a concealed handgun into courtrooms within the district, provided other means of security are employed.

The preservation of personal protection rights extended to knives. House Bill 2033 prohibits municipalities (excluding school districts, jails, and juvenile correctional facilities) from regulating transportation, possession, sales, transfers, gifting, licensing, registration, or uses of a knife or knife-making components. The bill also prohibits a municipality from passing ordinances that would be more restrictive regarding knife manufacturing than those for any other commercial product.

Schools

Education was a focal point for the legislature during 2013. Student behavior, protection of students from Internet materials, and curriculum issues were part of the education agenda.

Bullying

A bill was passed clarifying "bullying" to mean any threat by a student, staff member, or parent toward a student or staff member. The bill requires that these changes must be reflected in school districts' policies and plans.

Children's Internet Protection Act

House Bill 2109 requires schools and libraries to block access to any content with pictures showing sexual exploitation of children.

Curriculum

"Celebrate Freedom Week" designated the week of September 17 (or any other full school week as determined by the local school board) as "Celebrate Freedom Week," during which public schools are required to teach grades kindergarten through eight the history of the country's founding, with particular emphasis on the Declaration of Independence and the *U.S. Constitution*.

Although curriculum is usually the province of the State Department of Education, the Legislature was concerned that all citizens have knowledge of America's founding.

Innovative Districts

The Coalition of Innovative Districts Act, House Bill 2319, allowed up to ten percent of the state's school districts, at any one time, to opt out of most state laws, rules, and regulations to improve student achievement. The bill authorizes a process whereby a school district board of education may apply for authority to operate as a "public innovative district." Application and approval requirements are specified; the first two public innovative districts were selected in part by the governor and the chairpersons of the Senate and House education committees. The bill establishes the Coalition of Innovative Districts, the duties and functions of which are carried out by a Coalition Board. The Coalition Board consists of one representative of each public innovative district, chosen by the district's board. A public innovative district has authority to operate as such for five school years.

While the stated intent is to foster creativity, this bill also reflects the strong belief among some legislators that regulations of all types are suspect and should be eliminated.

State Budget

The 2014 budget bill made significant cuts in education at all levels as well as cuts for the judicial system, the highway fund, and elimination of 241 staff positions statewide. This slashed budget was necessary to pay for the huge income tax cuts passed in 2012.

For fiscal year 2014, the approved budget totaled $14.536 billion, including $5.964 billion from the State General Fund (SGF). Full-time equivalent (FTE) positions totaled 38,035.9, a decrease of 241.5 FTE positions (0.6 percent) below the governor's recommendation. The FY 2014 approved budget provides for an SGF ending balance of $521.2 million, or 8.7 percent of expenditures.

For fiscal year 2015, the approved budget totaled $13.925 billion—a cut from the 2014 budget. The FY 2015 approved budget provided for an ending balance of $678.9 million, (11.8 percent of expenditures). Among the approved adjustments to the governor's FY 2015 recommendations:

- The net deletion of $32.8 million in the budget of the State Board of Regents and the postsecondary education institutions, largely for salary reductions.
- The addition of $33.2 million in the Department of Education.
- The deletion of $38.3 million to reflect limits on the ability of agencies to expend funds for salaries and wages for FY 2015.

To save money, House Bill 2234 merged management of the Kansas Turnpike, which was independently funded and administered, with the Kansas Department of Transportation. The turnpike was financially healthy, and this bill tapped into this pot of money while streamlining the highway department as the governor proposed in his State of the State Address.

Taxes

The 2014 tax bill (House Bill 2059) reduced taxes for those in higher income tax brackets, raised taxes for lower income families, kept most of the sales tax, and eliminated some standard deductions, including mortgage deduction. The bill set the sales tax rate at 6.15 percent on July 1, 2013—down from 6.3 percent since 2010. The rate had been scheduled for reduction to 5.7 percent on July 1, 2013. Lowering taxes on individuals with higher incomes and on private enterprise was intended to be part of the plan to stimulate the economy and business growth, and retaining the higher sales tax was thought necessary to replace some of the revenue lost from the tax cuts for businesses passed in 2012.

The individual income tax rate for the bottom bracket for 2014 was reduced from 3.0 percent to 2.7 percent, and the top bracket of 4.9 percent was reduced to 4.8 percent. In tax year 2015, the top bracket was scheduled to be further reduced to 4.6 percent. The two rate brackets were set at 2.4 and 4.6 percent, respectively, in tax year 2016; 2.3 and 4.6 in tax year 2017; and 2.3 and 3.9 percent in tax year 2018.

A number of changes were enacted for itemized deductions. The deduction for certain gambling losses was repealed altogether. Most other itemized deductions (except the deduction for charitable contributions, which was fully retained) were reduced by 30 percent in tax year 2013; 35 percent in tax year 2014; 40 percent in tax year 2015; 45 percent in tax year 2016; and 50 percent in tax year 2017 and thereafter.

Kansas standard deduction levels for married taxpayers filing jointly and for single heads-of-household were reduced to $7,500 and $5,500 respectively, beginning in tax year 2013.

These changes were expected to increase tax receipts by approximately $308 million in fiscal year 2014 and by $777 million through the end of fiscal year 2018.

SESSION SUMMARY

Year three of Brownback's first term was a successful implementation of the governor's agenda. His tax program was embellished and several favorite issues of his supporters found a supportive legislature to pass their legislation. As a result of the 2012 tax cuts, the state budget trimmed education and other public services to address the impending revenue shortfall—if the economic boom from the tax cuts did not occur.

2014 STATE OF THE STATE ADDRESS

Governor Brownback launched the 2014 Legislative session with an address that first recalled some of the triumphs after he took office:

> Since December 2010, Kansas has added on average, more than a thousand private sector jobs every month and our unemployment rate has gone from 6.9 percent to 5.1 percent tied for the tenth lowest rate in the United States.
>
> We've put cash in the bank, we're paying our bills on time and we've balanced three budgets in a row. (Brownback 2014)

In this speech launching the 2014 legislative session, Brownback enumerated his priorities for the session:

- Ensure that every Kansas child has access to all-day kindergarten;
- Continue to support our universities and community and technical colleges;
- Build a state and an economy that works for everyone;
- Expand the Rural Opportunity Zones program;
- Allocate an additional $2 million to address the housing shortage, focused on moderate income housing;
- Provide money for the Rural Bridging Program to bring doctors to rural Kansas;
- Develop a comprehensive water strategy—a strategy to secure our water future for the next 50 years;
- Strengthen penalties for the most serious crimes by completing work on Hard 50 sentencing early in this session; and
- "Let us resolve that our schools remain open and are not closed by the courts or anyone else."

The last item is a reference to the Supreme Court's declarations that the state had not met its constitutional obligation to provide adequate and equitable funding for schools.

2014 LEGISLATIVE SESSION

The 2014 legislative session brought with it many bills that had been introduced during the 2013 session but either languished in committee or were not passed by both houses. Here we summarize the major bills, selected from a summary provided by the Kansas Legislative Research Department (2014). Once again, abortion, government deregulation, economic stimulation, and education were major issues. However, the governor's proposals for all-day kindergarten, addressing the housing shortage, and a strategy for water were not achieved.

Abortion

More legislation was passed to tighten controls on abortion in the state. Senate Bill 54 amends different statutes pertaining to abortion, adding or revising certain definitions to make them consistent, including statutes on licensing abortion facilities, medical emergencies involving abortion, abortions for minors, and abortions at facilities owned by the University of Kansas Hospital Authority.

Perhaps the most significant change in the existing law relates to the term "medical emergency," the description of which now eliminates references to "the best medical judgment of the attending physician and the determination of an emergency" in order to conform with the new definition of "medical emergency."

This bill seems to be somewhat complicated and convoluted, and the apparent purpose is to replace the judgment of the attending physician with the will of the legislature that abortion is never a good thing, and women should not have the right to choose abortion.

Deregulation

In its continuing effort to thwart federal domination, legislators passed and the governor signed Senate Substitute for House Bill 2051, a measure that objects to federal regulation of the Lesser Prairie Chicken. The federal government had issued regulations to forestall the demise of this bird that has been diminishing in number. Sensitivity to local control apparently did not apply to gun legislation (see "Gun Laws" below); such inconsistency in the perception of "local control" was a pattern in the Kansas Legislature during the Brownback years.

Another bill (HB 2549) permits the on-site disposal by underground burial of hazardous waste generated as the result of a cleanup approved by the Secretary of Health and Environment. And HB 2551 repeals the regulation of PCB disposal facilities and the atmospheric mercury deposition network. Because these two bills wantonly scuttle environmental safeguards, together they are examples of placing corporate profits above environmental safety and public health.

During the 2014 legislative session the House defeated an attempt to repeal the state's renewable energy standards, which had been passed by the Senate. Thus, the support for wind farms (wind is in abundance in Kansas) continues.

Economic Stimulation

As promised in Brownback's State of the State address, legislation was passed to stimulate the economy. House Bill 2430 is the Promoting Employment Across Kansas Act (PEAK), which made some changes in this program that gives new employers, or expanded businesses, a large percentage of its workers' state withholding tax. This bill extended for two years the period that employers could take the withheld tax, an adjustment because income taxes were cut in 2012. An amendment to increase workers' minimum wage to $10.10 per hour was ruled not germane to the bill.

Education

School funding was a major issue throughout the 2014 legislative session. A major piece of legislation passed was Senate Substitute for House Bill 2506, an appropriations bill drafted to meet the Supreme Court mandated $129 million increase in school funding, but ended with at least ten unrelated amendments. One of the amendments that caused a great deal of controversy was the elimination of teachers' due process if terminated. A reason given by legislators supporting the legislation is that tenure protects poor teachers.

Tenure is a contractual statement that after a probationary period, usually lasting three years, a teacher must be offered "due process," a formal impartial hearing, if a teacher's contract is terminated. The "due process" does not mean a teacher cannot be fired; it means that the administration must establish that the teacher has not met his or her professional responsibilities as a teacher.

The bill simply changed the definition of "teacher" when relating to due process. Previous to the implementation of this bill, a teacher was a professional who was required to hold a certificate to teach and was employed to provide instruction in Kansas. However, this bill defines "teacher" as any instructor in any technical college, the Institute of Technology at Washburn University, or community college; consequently, those employed to teach in public school through grade 12 are now excluded from due process.

In addition to allocating additional funding for schools, the appropriation bill changed the school finance formula to decrease various weightings to take effect in fiscal year 2015 and thereafter. For example, the funding formula no longer provided addition funding for pupils not eligible for the federal free lunch program but who failed to meet the standards established by the Kansas State Board of Education on either the mathematics or reading state assessments in the preceding school year. In addition, the definition of *at-risk pupil* was changed, excluding any pupil enrolled less than full time in grades one through 12 or any student over 19 years of age. These changes had the effect of pushing the additional costs of educating these students to the school district.

Because school funding had been a contentious issue between the Legislature and Supreme Court, this appropriations bill established a Pre-Kindergarten–Grade12 School Finance Study Commission to analyze the school finance system and school district spending, and to develop recommendations regarding the Legislature's constitutional funding obligations.

The school funding bill included a section that cut funding for implementation of the Common Core Standards. Most schoolteachers and administrators took a position articulated by School District #252 Superintendent Michael Argabright:

> We're going to move forward and not change College and Career Readiness Standards, Argabright stated. It was perceived that the Common Core was pushed onto us by the federal government. I don't think that's true at all. The State Board of Education made adjustments for Kansas. I applaud that. We are in our third year, and we've invested a lot of time and resources. Where people get lost in this issue—those are standards and we build curriculum around those standards. Building that curriculum around standards is very much local control. (Grover 2014)

A new law increased the maximum percentage of Kansas school districts that could operate as Public Innovative Districts from 10 percent to 20 percent. This bill authorized the additional 10 percent of school districts to operate as Public Innovative Districts if the school district operates a school within its district that is deemed to be either a Title I Focus School or a Title I Priority School. The innovative district law passed in 2013 enabled 10 percent of school districts to depart from many state regulations in order to offer innovative programs.

The Tax Credit for Low Income Students Scholarship Program Act provided eligible students with scholarships to pay all or a portion of tuition to attend a qualified school in Kansas. The scholarship is financed by a tax credit against corporate income tax liability beginning in tax year 2014 in an amount equal to 70 percent of the amount contributed for scholarships.

Another clause in the bill creates the Tax Credit for Low Income Students Scholarship Program. It provides "eligible students" with scholarships to pay all or a portion of tuition to attend a "qualified school" in Kansas.

A couple of definitions are needed here. An "eligible student" is a child who qualifies as an at-risk pupil—one who is eligible for free lunch and attends a school that would qualify as a Title I school. "Qualified school" is defined by the bill as any NONPUBLIC school providing education to elementary and secondary students. The only requirement is that the school must notify the State Board of Education of its intention to participate in the scholarship program. No standards are specified; no certification or supervision is required. And this is from a state that thrives on oversight in other services. This effort was another step toward the governor's and legislative leaders' efforts to move toward a privatized education system in the state.

Gun Legislation

Second amendment protection again was at the forefront of the legislature. House Bill 2140 allows in-state, off-duty and retired law enforcement officers, out-of-state law enforcement officers, and retired law enforcement officers to carry a concealed handgun in any building where an on-duty law enforcement officer is authorized to carry, including buildings lawfully prohibiting the concealed carry of firearms.

Legislation was passed that essentially eliminated local control of firearms and included such issues as federal transfer certifications, concealed carry by municipal employees, penalties for possession of a firearm under the influence, and disposal of seized weapons. House Bill 2578 specified the conditions for granting or denying federal firearm transfers, and when denied transfers can be appealed. This bill also created new prohibitions for municipalities related to the termination, demotion, discipline, and discrimination against concealed carry license holders, and records of employees' status as concealed carry license holders. It also established new posting requirements for certain public buildings and any private buildings where the open carrying of firearms might be restricted, and amended law regarding local government regulation of weapons, forfeiture and return of firearms, firearms buyback programs, and criminal use and possession of weapons.

Health Care

After one year of operation, KanCare (the privatized state health care system) participating insurance companies reported losses of $110 million, and payments to hospitals had been delayed. In response to complaints that processing claims was very slow, HB 2552 requires managed care organizations (MCOs) to fully pay or deny claims within 30 days after receipt and to fully pay or deny the allowed amount on all other claims within 90 days. The bill also subjects an MCO to fines for late payments and allows a provider with a claim that remains unpaid by an MCO after the applicable time limits to bring a direct cause of action against the MCO for the amount of the unpaid claim and interest. In addition, the bill prohibits the expansion of Medicaid eligibility without the approval of the Legislature.

A very controversial bill (HB 2553) would allow Kansas to join the Interstate Health Care Compact that would permit member states to regulate health care within their boundaries and to secure federal funding for health care. The Kansas Health Care Compact would result in the federal government issuing a block grant to Kansas to fund health care programs. Medicare would be included as a state-operated service. It was passed by the Kansas Legislature and signed by the governor in April 2014, but it would not become law in Kansas unless both the U.S. House of Representatives and Senate pass it.

Governor Brownback and most Republican legislators were strong critics of the 2010 federal Affordable Care Act, frequently called Obamacare, and supported HB 2553 to take a stand on federal intrusion in the state. The bill was written by ALEC (American Legislative Exchange Council), and eight other states had signed the compact before Kansas: Missouri, Oklahoma, Indiana, Texas, Georgia, Alabama, South Carolina, and Utah.

A related health care issue was the expansion of Medicaid to include more than 180,000 Kansans not receiving health care. Governor Brownback and leaders of the Kansas Legislature refused to pass legislation extending Medicaid to the poorest Kansans.

Judicial System

Shortly after his election Governor Brownback expressed strong misgivings about the Kansas Supreme Court. One concern was his belief that he should have more authority in the appointment of justices, and he stated publicly on numerous occasions that the court should have no role in school financing (even though such a role is written into the Kansas Constitution).

The existing system stipulated that a member of the Supreme Court would be appointed by the governor from a group of three candidates submitted by a nominating commission consisting of six lawyers selected by members of bar associations and five non-lawyers selected by the governor.

In March 2014 the Kansas Supreme Court issued a decision in the Gannon vs. Kansas suit on school finance. In this decision, the Supreme Court told the State that they are underfunding public education in Kansas. They told the State to immediately work to restore equitable funding for capitol outlay and local option supplemental aid across all 286 school districts in the state.

While the Supreme Court did the legislature a great favor by only ruling that poorer districts unable to raise local funds were underfunded and the deficiencies needed to be reduced by the state, they did not mandate a level of per-pupil funding. Nonetheless, the legislature apparently declared war on the court.

A constitutional amendment, HCR 5027, would require the Supreme Court nominating commission to forward to the governor the names of all qualified persons who submit their names to the commission for consideration, and to require the governor to appoint one of these people. The amendment would also require that a person deemed not qualified by the commission must be given a written statement of the reasons they were deemed unqualified. This resolution leaves the commission intact but expands the governor's choices for appointment; the resolution died in committee.

Senate Substitute for HB 2338 appropriates an additional $2 million from the State General Fund for the Judicial Branch, bringing its FY 2015 budget to $97,783,948. The bill allows the chief judge of a judicial district to submit a budget to the Chief Justice, beginning in fiscal year 2016. The Chief Justice has final authority over the annual amount allocated to each judicial district budget, but a chief judge making the elections has control of the expenditures under the budget except for salaries mandated by law.

The bill established that the district court judges in each district shall elect a district judge to serve as chief judge. Similarly, the judges of the Court of the Appeals shall elect one of their colleagues to serve as chief judge. Finally, the bill increased the time within which a judicial vacancy may be filled.

House Bill 2490 amended various statutes related to criminal sentencing. The bill establishes that a life sentence with a mandatory minimum term of imprisonment of 50 years (the "Hard 50" sentence) is the default sentence for a conviction of premeditated first degree murder committed on or after July 1, 2014. The sentencing judge may impose a "Hard 25" sentence if the judge finds substantial and compelling reasons to do so after reviewing mitigating circumstances.

Marriage

One constitutional amendment was introduced to define marriage. HCR 5026 proposed repeal of section 16 of article 15 of the state's constitution, which states that marriage shall be only between one man and one woman. Passage of this amendment would have opened the door to gay marriage, but this resolution died in a House committee.

Public Employees Retirement Fund

Senate Bill 423 granted the Department of Administration the authority to sell the Landon State Office Building, the Eisenhower State Office Building, the Curtis State Office Building and parking lot, and the Van Buren Project. The bill directs 80 percent of the proceeds from the sale of the properties to the Kansas Public Employees Retirement System (KPERS) for the purpose of reducing the unfunded liability. This decision to sell state assets to meet operating obligations was one of the early results of the 2012 tax cuts and an indicator of tight state budgets ahead.

House Bill 2533 changed the retirement plan for future tier 3 members of the Kansas Public Employees Retirement System (KPERS) plan implemented on January 1, 2015. This change includes most newly hired state, local, and public school employees. Provisions in the bill change the base year from 2016 to 2015 for calculation of interest credits; reduce the minimum guaranteed crediting rate from 5.25 percent to 4.0 percent; revise the formula for determining the additional discretionary interest credits; and revise the initial annuity interest rate credit of 6.0 percent at time of retirement to an interest rate equal to 2.0 percent less than the actuarial assumed investment rate.

In other words, these revisions reduce retirement benefits for future retirees.

State Budget

A concern for all school districts as they began the 2014 school year was the overall financial health of the state. School administrators were anticipating possible mid-year budget cuts because projected state spending was more than the anticipated revenue.

Duane Goossen (2014), Kansas Budget Director twelve years for the Governors Graves, Sebelius, and Parkinson put it this way: "The Kansas budget appears to be teetering on the edge of a fiscal cliff, but that's an illusion. We've already gone over the edge."

The Kansas Legislature approved a fiscal year 2015 budget that would spend $326 million more than the state expected to generate in revenue. That deficit would drain the state's bank account because revenue for FY 2014 fell $310 short of the anticipated amount.

As Goossen explained it, "Covering that $326 million difference almost completely drains the balance in the state's bank account. That brings us to the edge of the cliff. . . . With the bank balance tapped out, current year spending—already too meager in many areas like education—must be cut, and cut late in the fiscal year when it's difficult for agencies to make quick adjustments. That takes us over the cliff."

The 2014 budget passed by the legislature reflected little impact from the 2012–2013 tax cuts—that impact came later. The fiscal year 2014 budget (July 2013-June 2014) of $15.029 billion was a reduction of only $34.8 million and projected a State General Fund balance of $687.4 million, or 11.5 percent of state expenditures. However, the budget did forecast a decrease of $17.1 million for the funding of human services caseloads.

The budget total approved for fiscal year 2015 was $15.352 billion and provided for State General Fund balance of $365.9 million, or 5.8 percent of state expenditures. An important change in finances was the addition of $586.8 million allocated to the Department of Education from the deposit of the 20-mill property tax in the State Treasury. This money was formerly provided directly to local school districts. In other words, money that previously had been derived from property taxes and paid directly to local school districts, now was collected locally and sent to the State Treasury—so that it would be counted as state money spent on schools. This was a clever hocus-pocus that was never reported when the governor and other state leaders were describing the amount of money allocated for school funding from the state.

The closing of the legislative session, the "veto session," addressed no vetoes, but legislators passed a budget and several tax changes in the 79th day of the 2014 session; however, the fiscal health of the state came into question. Earlier in that week the Kansas Department of Revenue announced that April revenues were $92 million less than projected, adding some drama to the budget negotiations.

Governor Brownback's response during this election year was to blame the Obama administration for changes in the federal tax code. Let's review for a moment: Brownback's "roadmap for Kansas" was based on cutting corporate income taxes, a significant source of revenue, to stimulate economic growth with the promise that businesses would rush to Kansas with this business-friendly income tax plan. While nearby states were experiencing revenue increases and Kansas did not in 2014, some legislators and knowledgeable citizens were suspecting that there might possibly be some correlation between the Brownback tax plan and declining revenue.

Also, Moody's Investor Services announced that it was lowering the state's bond rating based on shrinking year-end balances, the reduced revenue from tax cuts in 2012 and 2013, and long-term pension obligations. With declining revenue and the state's 2014 spending pace, the state was expected to spend its $600 million reserve by 2016, according to projections developed by legislative fiscal analysts. This meant that the state could be forced to make more than $250 million in cuts to balance the budget by 2017.

Governor Brownback continued to insist that his roadmap for Kansas would lead the state to prosperity, despite road signs that portended either revamping the tax structure to supply more revenue or cutting spending and social programs. It was becoming apparent that the 2014 election would be a referendum on Brownback's leadership.

Taxes

House Bill 2643 allowed the classification of commercial and industrial machinery and equipment as personal property and provides guidelines for appraisers. This bill permits tax breaks for certain commercial interests and could result in a major tax hit for counties, continuing the Brownback program to favor corporate interests and to pass taxes to the local level. HB 2643 once again showed that Kansas government leaders wanted to give tax breaks to corporations, leaving citizens to pick up the tab for public services through property and sales taxes.

House Bill 2047 attacked local control by prohibiting municipalities, absent a majority vote and publication of such vote in official county newspapers, from approving annual budgets or other appropriations funded by increases in property taxes over the prior year that exceed the rate of inflation. A second provision of the bill requires all other municipalities, in response to increases in total tangible property valuation, to reduce the amount of most taxes levied to the prior year's level, absent a specifically allowed exception. This bill would require most municipalities that want to increase property taxes more than the rate of inflation that year to publicize the increase and to receive a majority vote by citizens.

A SENATOR REVIEWS THE LEGISLATIVE SESSION

Assessment of the 2014 Kansas Legislature's session and fiscal issues facing the state were topics during a conversation with Senator Jeff Longbine, who had been appointed to fill the Senate seat vacated by Jim Barnett in the fall of 2010. Longbine was elected to the Senate in 2012—the year that the governor collaborated with conservative leaders to purge several moderates—and was witness to the efforts by Governor Brownback to implement his "glide path to zero" taxes.

"We completed the session in 79 days, and that's got to be a highlight—11 days shorter than scheduled. I think it's the shortest session since 1994, and we had a school finance lawsuit that had to be dealt with," Longbine said (Grover and Calvert 2014).

Longbine said that the low point of the session was that a number of bills did not go through the whole legislative process, and he cited the teacher due process issue as an example. "There were a number of bills that passed one house but didn't get consideration in the other house and ended up in conference committee reports. I think there were times when we strayed away from the process that has served us very well. I'm not sure that the decorum was what it should have been at all times."

The due process amendment was actually put into the bill two days before it was voted on. "The House had a clean bill, and we [the Senate] ended up putting a number of policy measures in. One would be a credit on your property tax if you home-schooled or sent your kid to a nonpublic school. We had the corporate sponsorship that didn't eventually stay in. We had the due process piece. We had the defunding of Common Core, which was taken out, and there were a couple of others, including teacher licensure." He said the Budget Committee added some of those amendments, and some were inserted during floor debate.

Asked to assess the fiscal future for the state, Longbine said that many forecasting models had been run, and results depended upon the assumptions built into the models. One model that had received attention lately concluded that the state would face a deficit of $81 million in 2016, but that model assumed a revenue deficit of $200 million in 2014 and $100 million in 2015.

"We're not seeing growth in revenue; we're seeing decreases in revenue," he said. "Missing the revenue estimates last month was troubling, especially when you miss it by that far." April revenues were $92 million below projections.

CHAPTER SUMMARY

During Sam Brownback's first term the Kansas Legislature passed the governor's signature income tax cut, and the 2013 and 2014 sessions followed a 2012 election that brought a number of conservative legislators to augment the low-tax small-government model of Brownback.

The 2013 legislative session was a successful implementation of the governor's agenda. His tax program was embellished and several favorite issues of his supporters found a supportive legislature to pass their legislation. As a result of the 2012 tax cuts, the state budget trimmed education and other public services to address the impending revenue shortfall—if the economic boom from the tax cuts did not occur.

By the end of Brownback's second term, the impact of the drastic tax cuts were beginning to appear; state revenue was not reaching expected levels. The drama of the 2014 governor's election had begun, and Sam Brownback's programs were before the voting public.

REFERENCES

Associated Press. 2012a. "Brownback Iowa-bound to Stump for Perry." *Associated Press State Wire*, Kansas (KS), January 2.

Associated Press. 2012b. "Brownback Reacts to Boeing Kansas Decision." *Associated Press State Wire*, Kansas (KS), January 4.

Brownback, Sam. 2013. "Kansas Is a Special Place; 2013 State of the State Address." *Kansas State Library*. https://kslib.info/DocumentCenter/View/1151/Sam-Brownback---State-of-the-State-Address-2013.

Brownback, Sam. 2014. "A Kansas Renaissance; 2014 State of the State Address." *Kansas State Library*. https://kslib.info/395/Speeches.
Carpenter, Tim. 2011a. "Brownback Adds to Cabinet." *Topeka Capital-Journal*, January 4.
Carpenter, Tim. 2011b. "Kansas Conservatives Prepare to Strike Social Conservatives in Control; Republicans Have opportunity to Reshape Issues of the State." *Topeka Capital-Journal*, January 9.
Carpenter, Tim. 2011c. "Brownback Squeezing Mental Health Funding." *Topeka Capital-Journal*, January 17.
Carpenter, Tim. 2011d. "Brownback: Job Growth Key to Reforms." *Topeka Capital-Journal*, January 20.
Carpenter, Tim. 2011e. "Brownback Signs Major Abortion Bills." *Topeka Capital-Journal,* April 12.
Carpenter, Tim. 2011f. "Legislature Passes New State Budget." *Topeka Capital-Journal*, May 12.
Carpenter, Tim. 2012. "Brownback Signs Large State Tax Cut." *Topeka Capital-Journal*, May 22.
Cooper, Brad. 2012a. "Bill Comes Due for Tax Cuts." *Kansas City Star*, December 5.
Cooper, Brad. 2012b. "Graves and Brownback Take Opposite Sides in Kansas GOP Primary." *Kansas City Star*, July 10.
Cooper, Brad. 2012c. "Voila, Smaller Government." *Kansas City Star*, December 30.
Editors. 2011a. "What Others Are Saying—Brownback Isn't Making Friends." *Kansas City Star*, January 16.
Editors. 2011b. "Editorial: Speed Limit Change Reasonable." *Topeka Capital-Journal*, April 12.
Editors. 2012a. "The Star's Editorial—Kansas Medicaid Reform Must Protect the Needy." *Kansas City Star*, January 2.
Editors. 2012b. "Brownback Reverses Course on Primary Endorsements." *Topeka Capital-Journal*, July 13.
Eligon, John. 2013. "Kansas' Governor and G.O.P. Seek to End Income Tax." *New York Times*, January 23.
Goossen, Duane. 2014. "Don't Believe the Revenue Estimates — Kansas' Budget Has Already Gone Off the Fiscal Cliff." *The Kansas Budget* (blog), July 22, 2014. http://www.kansasbudget.com/2014/07/dont-believe-revenue-estimates-kansas.html.
Grover, Bob. 2014. "School Funding Bill Disappoints." *Emporia Gazette,* May 2.
Grover, Bob, and Jim Calvert. 2014. "Longbine Reviews Legislative Session." *Emporia Gazette,* May 16.
Hanna, John. 2012. "Kan. Senate Reverses Course to Approve Tax Cuts." *Deseret News,* March 21.
Kansas City Star. 2012a. "Brownback Signs Big Tax Cut in Kansas." *Kansas City Star*, May 23.
Kansas City Star. 2012b. "Brownback's Ominous Remake of Kansas." *Kansas City Star,* December 27.

Kansas Legislature. *2013 Summary of Legislation*. Topeka, KS: Kansas Legislative Research Department, August. http://www.kslegresearch.org/KLRD-web/Publications/SummaryofLegislation/2013_summary_of_legislation.pdf.

Kansas Legislature. *2014 Summary of Legislation*. Topeka, KS: Kansas Legislative Research Department, July. http://www.kslegresearch.org/KLRD-web/Publications/SummaryofLegislation/2014_summary_of_legislation.pdf/.

Klepper, David. 2011a. "Kansas Lawmakers to Face Same Money Woes, but Different Answers are Likely." *Kansas City Star*, January 2.

Klepper, David. 2011b. "Repeal of Kansas Sales Tax Increase Could Be Hot Topic for New Legislature." *Kansas City Star*, January 3.

Klepper, David. 2011c. "Brownback Budget Won't Make Up for Lost School Stimulus Money." *Kansas City Star*, January 13.

Loomis, Burdett. 2011. "Consolidation of Power a Concern." *Wichita Eagle*, May 1.

Marso, Andy. 2012. "School Finance Plan to Face Session Scrutiny." *Topeka Capital-Journal*, January 6.

Milburn, John. 2011. "Deeper State Budget Cuts Will Hit Schools Again." *Wichita Eagle*, January 3.

Schremmer, Mark. 2011. "GOP Plans Long-term." *Topeka Capital-Journal*, January 3.

Smith, Michael A. 2012. "Insight Kansas: Unsticking a State Stuck on Redistricting." *Pittsburg Morning Sun*, April 24.

Smith, Michael A. 2016. "Insight Kansas: Are You Better Off than You Were Four Years Ago?" *Hays Post*, September 30.

Chapter 6

2014 Election Becomes a Referendum on the Experiment

CHAPTER OVERVIEW

Sam Brownback had been in the governor's office for three years, and 2014 was an election year. He had begun implementation of his "great experiment" in 2012 with major tax cuts that were intended to give the Kansas economy "a shot of adrenalin." This year would be pivotal to his governorship, and his reelection was essential to continue implementation of his plan, which became the focus of the campaign for governor.

Democratic candidate Paul Davis claimed that the experiment was a failure, and Brownback energetically defended his plan that was supported by the Kansas Legislature. The outcome of the election would be a measure of the experiment's acceptance by the public and pivotal to continuation of Brownback's plan for the state.

VULNERABLE INCUMBENTS

The Democrats nominated Kansas House Minority Leader Paul Davis for governor in 2014. Davis hailed from Lawrence, the home of the University of Kansas, widely regarded as the most liberal city in the state. Davis, an attorney, had the right connections for fundraising. He was also polished on the stump. Democrats were quick to anoint him as the right one to challenge Brownback, and no other Democrat mounted a serious challenge. In fact, Democrats in Kansas rarely had a competitive primary until 2018, four years later. Davis quickly rose to being the standard-bearer challenging Brownback.

Brownback had a dark horse primary challenger, but no moderate Republican opponent. This is somewhat of a surprise, because Brownback was closely associated with the conservative wing of the state Republican Party, plus he had those low popularity ratings. However, Brownback also had his state and national fundraising connections from the time when he was a U.S. senator. As a result, he was able to raise a great deal of money and quickly secure the endorsement of the Kansas Chamber of Commerce, which is strongly supported by Charles and David Koch. Thus, no strong moderate Republican emerged to challenge Brownback in the primaries. The dark-horse candidate, Jennifer Winn, had no statewide name recognition and raised little money, yet she was still able to muster 95,000 votes in the GOP primary, which commentators also took to be a bad sign for the governor (Roy 2014).

Instead of backing a moderate primary challenger, a long list of former elected officials who were moderate Republicans endorsed Davis in the general election cycle. One conservative commentator, former Kansas House Speaker Doug Mays responded that he was very surprised by the endorsements. Known for his acerbic wit, Mays quipped that he was surprised because "I thought many of them had died."

There was one more competitive, statewide election in 2014. Pat Roberts was Kansas' senior U.S. senator, elected back in '96. Previously, Roberts, now in his 80s, was reelected easily. In 2008 Roberts secured more than 60 percent of the vote against ex-Congressman Jim Slattery, while in 2002, he had only a Libertarian opponent, and won over 80 percent of the vote. Roberts looked safe yet again, this time with the focus on the governor's race, plus Kansans are less apt to vote for Democrats in national-level elections. Kansas' last Democratic U.S. Senator was defeated for reelection in 1938.

Roberts started the campaign cycle looking like an easy reelection win. However, an insurgent campaign from a Republican challenger shook things up. Milton Wolf, a doctor from Johnson County, broke through with a novel commercial. The humorous commercial featured a Roberts' look-alike sitting on a recliner, on a golf course. The point being made in the commercial, which also featured a voiceover, was that Pat Roberts did not live in Kansas. For all purposes except representation in the Senate, Roberts' home address was a house in the Virginia suburbs of Washington, DC. When it came to his Senate representation, Roberts used the address of a local supporter. This supporter happened to live in a community near a golf course, and the recliner-on-a-golf-course image became iconic in the 2014 campaign. The phrase "Pat Roberts does not live in Kansas" also became lore. Roberts defeated Wolf after revelations that Wolf, a doctor, had posted patients' X-Ray images on social media without their permission, but he still had to face independent candidate Greg Orman, a Johnson County entrepreneur.

Democrats sensed an opportunity in the Orman-Roberts race. Orman launched his campaign with some of his own money, stressing his status as an independent, not an affiliate of the party. Democrats had a different take.

They saw Orman's wild card candidacy as an opportunity. Democrats had put in a candidate of their own for the Senate, Chad Taylor, but he was raising little money and appeared to be largely there as a placeholder. Democrats sued the office of Kansas Secretary of State Kris Kobach to remove Taylor from the ballot. Kansas law generally stipulates that if anyone filed in that party's primary, then that party must put forth a candidate and not remove that person's name from the ballot unless there is a compelling reason. Kobach argued that the Democrats did not meet the test for removing their candidate's name from the ballot, unless perhaps they were willing to appoint someone else. However, Kansas state courts ruled in favor of the Democrats. Taylor's name was removed from the ballot for the U.S. Senate seat and not replaced. Orman was the only person challenging Roberts in the general election.

The Democrats, and most observers, believed that Orman was running as a de facto Democrat. However, a few years later, Orman would release his book, *A Declaration of Independents*, in which he claimed that it was his independence, not his being a de facto Democratic candidate, that led his vote totals in 2014. As this book goes to press, Orman also filed as an independent in the 2018 Kansas governor's race despite many Democrats' concerns that he will act as a spoiler candidate.

Roberts went into the general election running on his experience, while Orman stressed themes of new blood and independence. Like Wolf, Orman hit Roberts for not living in Kansas.

Sam Brownback's popularity ratings were low, according to public opinion polls going into the 2014 election cycle. At some point in his first term, Brownback's popularity ratings dipped below 40 percent (Flentje 2014). As of October, 54 percent of Kansans polled disapproved of his performance as governor (Cooper 2014). As a result, many observers predicted it would be a competitive election. Kansas is a heavily Republican state, as measured by its electoral vote in the presidential election, which has not gone to a Democrat since 1964. However, state and local elections here can be highly competitive. Since Kansas' Republican Party split into rival moderate and conservative factions starting in the late 1980s, Democrats could pick up seats in state and local elections, and even a few congressional races, when the Republicans nominated candidates that were perceived as too far to the right. The 2014 election seemed to fit that mold very well.

BROWNBACK ENTERS THE RACE

Very early in the campaign for governor was a $500,000 contribution controversy. In January 2014 *The Kansas City Star* (Helling and Cooper 2014) reported that Lieutenant Governor Jeff Colyer had loaned $500,000 to

Governor Sam Brownback's reelection campaign. The amount was reportedly a record for Kansas elections. In that same article, the authors noted that the large contribution, while legal, was significant in a political sense. Before that donation, the Brownback and Davis campaigns each had collected about $1.1 million in contributions during 2013, and the loan may have been intended to avoid the appearance that the Brownback campaign was not doing well. Helling and Cooper quoted coauthor of this book Michael Smith: "When you're in Brownback's position—a Republican governor in a Republican state—the perception that a Democrat has pulled even with you is no good."

Brownback formally entered the governor's race in May 2014. The campaign was launched with Brownback accompanied by his two campaign co-chairs, former U.S. senator Bob Dole and Mary Eisenhower, a granddaughter of President Dwight Eisenhower. At the campaign announcement event in the State Capitol, Brownback highlighted his conservative credentials:

> I want to keep our Kansas renaissance going. Now, my opponent wants to follow the current federal government model—raise taxes, implement Obamacare and put us on the same downward spiral. I say no. (Carpenter 2014a)

With Lieutenant Governor Jeff Colyer as his running mate, Brownback declared, "Kansas now leads where once we lagged. We have jobs, new construction, technical education growth and new start-up businesses."

However, a report published that same month cast doubts on the success of the Brownback economic program in Kansas. The Nelson A. Rockefeller Institute of Government at the State University of New York reported that Kansas was among 10 states with revenue declines for the first half of fiscal year 2014. Of those states, Kansas had the second-greatest decline (Cooper 2014). Furthermore, April tax collections fell $93 million short of estimates, and state revenues were down $480 million for the first three quarters of the 2014 fiscal year. This revenue decline was credited by many to the 2012 tax cuts promoted by Brownback and supported by the conservative Kansas legislature.

The bad news continued the next month. Duane Goossen, budget director for the three governors who preceded Brownback, said that he did not believe the state would be able to implement the budget for fiscal year 2015 passed by legislators the previous month. "I don't think there's going to be enough money in the bank for the state to make it all the way through fiscal year 2015 and cover the budget that has been approved," Goossen said. "Something is going to have to happen already now in this (coming) fiscal year to keep the state balanced and keep the checkbook above zero" (Marso 2014).

Combined April and May revenues were more than $300 million below projections, supporting Goossen's prediction that the decreasing revenue stream would not sustain the legislature's budget. This troubling financial trend was very much in the minds of candidates as the campaign season of 2014 began.

THE RACE UNFOLDS

Polls were looking good for both Orman and Davis going into the 2014 general election. Both races were generally within the margin of error on tracking polls, and some even showed each of them in the lead. These were amazing performances for a Democrat and an independent candidate, respectively, both challenging Republican incumbents in Kansas. Money came forth, and the resulting television commercials were notable. Brownback was widely ridiculed for a television commercial in which he stated that "the sun is shining in Kansas, and don't let anyone tell you different." Observers were quick to point out the state's difficult budget situation, which the conventional wisdom pinned on Brownback, more specifically the tax cut. "The sun is shining in Kansas" became a popular joke.

For his part, Davis countered with a commercial in which his campaign staff hired a stunt driver to drive a car backward with Davis sitting in the passenger seat, talking to the camera. Davis' point was that Brownback's policies were taking Kansas backward. On the stump and on TV, Davis generally stressed his support for education, specifically the school base funding formula, which had lost money under the tax cut and was criticized by Brownback and his supporters. Davis' "backward" commercial was memorable. However, it was not decisive.

With the legislative session behind, Governor Brownback during the summer of 2014 turned his attention to his reelection. Governor Brownback frequently claimed during his campaign that he had increased funding for education and improved the pension system for teachers. He frequently made the statement that strengthening public schools was one of his primary goals.

However, an examination of one medium-sized school district is a case study in the school funding situation during the early Brownback years in Kansas. Robert Scheib, Assistant Superintendent of Business for Emporia Unified School District #253, told one of the authors that funding for the Emporia School District in 2014–15 was down $3.6 million from 2008 (Grover 2014).

Also, the Base State Aid Per Pupil (BSAPP) for 2014–15 was $3,852—*down* from $4,492 required by statute but *up* $14 from $3,838 allocated in 2013–14. Is that the "more" that the governor spoke of? Even that $14 increase in Base State Aid Per Pupil was not a real increase. "The $14 [increase] goes in and comes right back out with the $40,000 for at-risk students that we lose," Scheib said. "We got $14 in one hand; then they took it with the other hand." In the 2014 school-funding bill, funding for at-risk students was reduced for part-time students and for those who don't qualify for free lunch but are not "proficient"—students who don't do well on state proficiency tests.

Perhaps the governor based his claim on "more funding" on this funding change: twenty mills of local levy that school districts in the past deposited in local banks and drew interest on, now went to the state. The state earned interest on this money, kept the interest, and sent the original amount back to the school districts as state aid. "We get a check from the county treasurer for 33 mills," Scheib explained. "The county treasurer also makes out a check to the state for 20 mills, and they deposit it. It's a half-billion dollars statewide."

For the Emporia school district, this returned local funding amounted to $3 million that the governor claimed as state funding for Emporia schools. And the state earned interest on local tax money deposited and held short term by the state.

Even with the gimmick of returning locally generated property tax money to local schools and calling it "state aid," the claim that the state "increased funding in record amounts" is disputed by the authors and most observers familiar with school funding in Kansas.

In addition to the funding of schools, the financial health of the state was being questioned by Democrats and by those knowledgeable of state finances. During its 2014 session the Kansas Legislature approved a fiscal year (FY) 2015 budget that spent $326 million more than the state expected to generate in revenue. Even during the 2014 election campaign it was apparent that the deficit would drain the state's bank account because revenue for FY 2014 fell $310 million short of the anticipated amount.

Duane Goossen, Kansas Budget Director twelve years for the Graves, Sebelius, and Parkinson administrations, put it this way: "Covering that $326 million difference almost completely drains the balance in the state's bank account. That brings us to the edge of the cliff. . . . With the bank balance tapped out, current year spending—already too meager in many areas like education—must be cut, and cut late in the fiscal year when it's difficult for agencies to make quick adjustments. That takes us over the cliff" (Goossen 2014a).

During the 2014 election campaign the governor and other leaders in the Legislature were reluctant to mention the looming possibility of cuts to education and other programs that served the people. Then in August—less than three months before the election—Standard and Poor's joined Moody's in lowering the bond rating for Kansas, providing additional evidence that the governor's "great experiment" for Kansas was failing, taking education and the state's bond rating down with it. Standard and Poor's and Moody's are the two largest bond rating agencies in the U.S., and their ratings often serve as benchmarks to investors, policymakers, and one another.

DISSENSION AMONG REPUBLICANS

Opposition to the Brownback agenda was not restricted to Kansas Democrats. During the summer months of 2014, a number of prominent Republicans went public with their dissent of Brownback and openly supported Paul Davis, the Democratic candidate for governor. In July *The Topeka Capital-Journal* reported that more than 100 Republican leaders and activists publicly announced their support for Davis. Wint Winter, a former state senator, reflected the thoughts of many:

> All of us are proud Republicans. We came together because of our common love of Kansas, our commitment to Kansas families and our belief in moderate, common sense leadership. We are deeply concerned by the direction Sam Brownback is taking Kansas. (Carpenter 2014b)

A list of 104 Republicans campaigning against Brownback included three former State Senate Presidents, three former House Speakers, two former Lieutenant Governors, a former U.S. Representative, a prior Kansas GOP chairman, the current Kansas Insurance Commissioner, plus a number of national GOP delegates, local school board members, mayors, and city and county officials. Clearly, there was not unanimity among the Republican Party leadership.

Former Senate President Dick Bond, a Republican, issued the following stinging statement:

> Kansans know that Sam Brownback will try to distract and mislead throughout this campaign. He wants to blame the mess in Kansas on Barack Obama . . . . From our stalled economy to his ill-advised tax policy to our struggling schools—to the Kansas drought. But the only person to blame for this mess is Sam Brownback. (Carpenter 2014b)

In the same newspaper report, state Republican Party Chair Kelly Arnold provided his reaction to the dissenters within his party:

> The Kansas Republican Party is disappointed these former elected officials, many of whom were thrown out by the Kansas voters, have decided to endorse the Obama agenda.

Brownback had contributed to the split between conservatives and moderates in the Kansas Republican Party by openly campaigning against moderates in the 2012 election. Conservatives won enough seats during that election to take control of the Senate; conservatives already controlled the House. Consequently, Brownback had significant support for his efforts to conduct his "experiment" of small government and low taxes. Among the policies passed were the tax cuts and reduced state income, blocked expansion of Medicaid, reduced funding of education, and tapping of highway funds to fund state services.

About the same time that some Kansas Republican leaders announced their opposition to the Brownback agenda, former U.S. senator Rick Santorum, a Pennsylvania Republican, endorsed Brownback. Santorum had served with Brownback in the U.S. Senate. Santorum joined former U.S. Senate Majority Leader and presidential candidate Bob Dole, who had earlier announced his support of Brownback.

It should be noted that approximately 25 percent of Kansas voters were registered Democrats, 46 percent were Republicans, and Independents outnumbered Democrats. Keen Umbehr was the Libertarian Party's nominee for governor.

ISSUES RAISED BY BROWNBACK'S OPPONENT, PAUL DAVIS

During an interview, attorney Paul Davis, then minority leader of the Kansas House of Representatives, stressed his concern for public education as a key for the state's economic future. Asked why he wanted to be governor, Davis responded,

> I think the state is really going in the wrong direction in a number of different ways right now. We've got to get the state going back in the right direction so we can see the kind of growth all Kansans want to see. It starts with making sure we have the very best public schools, and we've got to restore the cuts to public schools. That's really my top priority as governor—restore the cuts that have been made to our public schools because I think stronger public schools are the foundation for a stronger economy. (Grover and Calvert 2014a)

Davis went on to state that despite Brownback's promise that his tax cuts would lead to a shot of adrenaline to the economy, Kansas had not seen the record growth he promised. Davis noted that the state's credit rating had been downgraded three times in a year. Furthermore, he pointed out that the Kansas economy was trailing that of neighboring states and that of the nation.

"We're in big trouble, and the Brownback experiment has failed," Davis said. "Consequently, we're making huge cuts to schools that don't just affect kids today, but their careers and future livelihoods."

Davis said that as governor he would immediately address Brownback's income tax cuts.

"To borrow from the old adage, 'When you're in a hole, the first thing you need to do is stop digging,'" he began. "The governor's tax plan is going to result in a huge budget deficit over the next five years. Our Legislative Research Department, which is nonpartisan and always has been relied upon for good numbers, projects a $1.3 billion deficit."

He then revealed his plan for addressing that deficit:

> What we have put on the table is that we need to freeze the income tax rates where they're going to be on January 1 of 2015 so that we can prevent the massive deficits that we're going to see. Then we need to get back to restoring the cuts to public schools.

Davis also proposed creation of a tax commission to examine the tax code as a whole and make recommendations for future action. He said that he would follow the deliberate strategies of previous governors; he would involve Kansans—economists, community leaders, and business leaders.

He compared his plan with Brownback's approach. "I think it's a real contrast to what Governor Brownback did because what he decided to do was hire Art Laffer and pay him $75,000 in taxpayers' money to design this plan. He did it without involving Kansans in the discussion. That's just not the way to go about tax policy."

During that interview with governor candidate Paul Davis, he outlined his position on health care, judicial appointments, and leadership (Grover and Calvert 2014b).

Asked his position on Medicaid expansion, he responded by saying that he has spent a lot of time over the past year listening to hospital administrators, nursing home administrators, physicians, home health agencies, and Medicaid beneficiaries.

"I've become convinced that this is a critical issue for all of those folks," Davis said. "A lot of hospitals are really getting squeezed right now. I've had many conversations with rural hospital administrators in particular about why they believe this is critical to their very existence. They're not sure they can stay in business if they don't have Medicaid expansion."

In addition, expanding Medicaid would help the Kansas economy. "It would also inject several billion dollars into the state economy and create a lot of jobs," Davis added. "It's our tax dollars we're paying into the federal government, and if we don't get them back, they're just going to some other state."

A related healthcare issue was the state's participation in the Health Care Compact passed by both houses and signed by the governor during the 2014 session—an agreement among eight states to receive federal healthcare funds as block grants and to distribute them in each state. Asked his opinion of the

Health Care Compact, Davis responded, "The health care compact is something that ought to concern everybody who is Medicare eligible and is going to be Medicare eligible because it very specifically allows the state to take over the Medicare program, which I think would be a huge mistake."

Also, Brownback had proposed changing the process for selecting Supreme Court justices, eliminating the commission that forwards three nominees for the governor to make a selection.

Asked why Kansans should vote for him and his running mate Jill Docking, Davis replied, "All of these issues and many others that are facing the state we're going to need to come together as Democrats and Republicans to address these issues. I don't believe that all of the good ideas are in one party or the other."

STATE FAIR DEBATE DELINEATED CANDIDATES' STANDS ON ISSUES

As the election drew nearer, Democratic gubernatorial candidate Paul Davis was leading Brownback in polls—surprising in a Republican state that had elected Brownback by a large margin just four years prior.

At a September debate during the State Fair in Hutchinson, the two major party candidates for governor defined their platforms. Both candidates focused on Brownback's "great experiment" which included significant cuts in business and personal income taxes. Davis pledged to freeze future income tax cuts to stabilize the Kansas economy and to increase funding for education, his highest priority. Brownback insisted that the tax cuts were performing as planned—encouraging business expansion and creating new jobs.

Brownback several times referred to Davis as a liberal who supported President Barack Obama. Brownback said he opposed expanding Medicaid health insurance to the state's poorer residents because it meant implementing Obamacare.

Davis accused Brownback of using Kansas as an ideological laboratory, and Davis would support Medicaid expansion as some Republican governors had. Davis introduced himself as "a moderate and an independent thinker" who opposes the governor's cuts to education and pledged to restore those cuts as "my very top priority" if elected governor. He reiterated that his first priority is education. He also attacked the governor's proclaimed economic "experiment" of low taxes to spur the economy:

> The governor's experiment just isn't working. We're trailing our surrounding states and the rest of the country in just about every economic indicator. We're in debt—nearly $1.3 billion over the next 3 years. He's jeopardizing our schools

> and our future. We can do better. This election presents a clear choice—whether we're going to restore cuts to our public schools and get this state moving again or whether we're going to hit the accelerator on a failed economic experiment. (Kansas State Fair Debate 2014)

Brownback responded that his opponent was wrong. "There are more Kansans working now than ever in the history of the state. We put more money into education than ever in the history of the state."

The candidates' closing statements summarized their campaign positions that they would convey to the voters. Brownback said that his running mate, Jeff Colyer, and he wanted two things: (1) To make Kansas the best place in America to raise a family and (2) to support business and "we're a long ways along the path to do that." He vowed that they would continue to "push that model" and he insisted that the state "is on the right track now." He wanted Kansans' kids and grandkids to move back to the state—a place with a "great future." He concluded, "There's no place better to watch a sunset. There's no place better to have a family. There's no place better to live than Kansas. And we're going to make it even better."

Davis began his concluding statement by reiterating that the state is "not headed in the right direction. The experiment is not working, and it's not going to work." He claimed that the result was "damaging schools, hurting the economy. It's jeopardizing our future." He then turned to his personal qualifications to be governor and his support by "over a hundred current and former elected officials." Finally, he said, "If you believe we need a governor who will put the people of Kansas before his own personal political agenda, I ask for your support. I'm a lifelong Kansan. I'm a moderate. I'm an independent thinker. I'm a commonsense leader. Together we can get our state back on the right track."

SEX, DRUGS, AND MURDER: BROWNBACK'S LATE CAMPAIGN MOVES

With the election looking competitive according to the polls, the parties and various other third-party and independent organizations began pouring in the money. A few years earlier, the *Citizens United* U.S. Supreme Court ruling had determined that there was no limit on independent expenditures in political campaigns when they are made by individuals, corporations, or labor unions. An additional U.S. Supreme Court ruling applied *Citizens United* to state as well as federal elections. The two gubernatorial candidates raised and spent roughly equal amounts of money: 4.7 million dollars for Brownback versus 4.6 million for challenger Davis (Campaign Finance Institute 2019). However, there were other factors in play.

With Roberts facing a far more formidable opponent than he had in years, nearly $17 million flowed into that race (Associated Press 2014). Republicans used the money well. According to political science professor Chapman Rackaway,

> From voter files to interest group connections, and from campaign plans to staffing, the Kansas Republican party has been a support network for the legion of candidates. . . . Moderate Republicans and Democrats, by contrast, were either completely disorganized (the moderate GOP members), or playing catch-up (Democrats) with the new GOP machine in Topeka. (Rackaway 2015)

While Orman stressed independence and new blood, hitting Roberts on his nonresidency and refusal to answer questions, Davis emphasized support for education funding and criticized Brownback for the tax cuts and resulting budget problems. The Republicans, on the other hand, had nearly identical themes until the end. Brownback, Roberts, and the groups running ads on their behalf all sought to nationalize the races by labeling Orman and Davis as liberals and tying them to national Democratic leaders such as U.S. House Minority Leader Nancy Pelosi and Senate Minority Leader Harry Reid. They often pointed out the out-of-state money flowing to the two challengers from supporters with ties to Pelosi, Reid, and other Democrats. Roberts insisted that Orman was actually a Democrat, not an independent. The word "liberal" was bandied about a lot by Brownback, Roberts, and the independent expenditures being made on their behalf. Davis' hometown and profession even gave rise to a meme: the three L's, aka the Liberal Lawyer from Lawrence.

Davis, Roberts, and Orman all generally stuck to the same themes through Election Day. Brownback and his supporters, on the other hand, made some last-minute attacks against Davis. The Republican Governor's Association ran a series of last-minute ads arguing that Paul Davis was inside a strip club when it was raided for drugs in 1998. Davis, who was single in '98, did not deny being in the back room with a scantily clad woman, but authorities said that he was not suspected of any wrongdoing regarding drugs (Cooper 2014).

Brownback himself also made a late move in the campaign, trying to tie Davis to a horrific murder case from Wichita. Brothers Jonathan and Reginald Carr had been convicted of a particularly horrible massacre in Wichita, brutally murdering five people over several days in 2000. They were sentenced to death penalty, despite the fact that Kansas has not carried out an execution since the 1960s. The Kansas Supreme Court upheld the conviction but ordered a re-sentencing due to procedural problems at the first trial. Ultimately, the Carr Brothers were sentenced to live in prison without parole or probation.

A group outraged by the Kansas Supreme Court's actions had mobilized to reject two of the judges on the ballot for retention, both of whom had voted for the re-sentencing. Kansas uses the merit selection, or Missouri nonpartisan court plan, in which the governor appoints judges to fill vacancies based on a list submitted by members of the Bar in good standing. Those judges then sit for periodic retention elections, and are nearly always retained in office.

The argument for non-retention ignored the legalities of the Carr Brothers case, instead focusing on the longstanding "soft on crime" argument often thrown at elected officials and judges. With just days to go before the election, Brownback announced that he would vote "no" on the retention of Judges Eric Rosen and Lee Johnson due to the Carr Brothers case, and accused Davis of being soft on crime. Davis, who had known one of the massacre victims since high school, responded with anger. There is little indication that the issue had much traction outside Wichita, but it may have made a difference there. In the end, Rosen and Johnson were retained, but by far smaller margins than usual (Biles 2014).

By October, the race for the governorship was very close. Monmouth University in New Jersey published a poll that gave Davis a five-percentage point lead over Brownback. Several polls during the last weeks before the election showed the race tied. New Jersey Governor Chris Christie visited Kansas four times in support of Brownback, and the Republican Governors Association was airing ads attacking Davis (Shorman 2014).

As the election neared, the race tightened even more—a notable contrast to the 2010 governor's race won by Brownback with 63 percent of the vote. He viewed his margin of victory as a mandate for change and consequently implemented his plan to cut income taxes, reduce aid to the arts, privatize Medicaid, sign abortion restrictions, and eliminate tenure for K–12 teachers. However, despite predictions that the huge tax cuts would stimulate economic growth, by the time of the election, state tax revenue had fallen below predictions five of the preceding seven months.

Bob Beatty, professor of political science at Washburn University, stated, "The governor's election is a referendum on everything about Sam Brownback—from A to Z (Carpenter 2014c)." Both Paul Davis and Libertarian Party nominee Keen Umbehr in their campaigns claimed that Brownback's term as governor was an experiment gone bad. In the days before the election Insight Kansas, a polling aggregation project at Washburn University, produced polling results that showed Davis with an average lead of three points over Brownback (Carpenter 2014c). An upset win by Davis seemed possible.

ELECTION RESULTS

In the end, Brownback and Roberts both won. Brownback defeated Davis by less than 4 percent. Roberts' margin was wider—he bested Orman by just over 10 points.

Polls had both races within the margin of error going into Election Day. What happened?

Ultimately, Davis would have won the election had it not been for the lightly populated, but very Republican counties of Western Kansas. Most Kansans live east of Salina, and Davis won that territory. However, he did not win Johnson County, the state's wealthiest, most populous, and most vote-rich county. However, Johnson County usually goes Republican, and Davis did keep it close. He won the state's small Democratic base in Lawrence and in Wyandotte County. He won many swing counties such as Lyon County, location of Emporia, and Crawford County, location of Pittsburg, both small college towns. Lyon and Crawford counties are about as close to Ohio or Florida as Kansas gets. They are both "purple." They are counties that served as bellwethers.

One thing that is notable about the 2014 election in Kansas is the fact the tracking polls were off, over-measuring support for the Democrat and the Independent. This is eerily similar to the problem with tracking polls in the 2016 presidential election, in which many observers predicted a Hillary Clinton victory, but it was not to be (Smith 2017). Whatever systematic or accidental biases existed in these polls, Kansas may have been a harbinger of what was to come two years later. Apparently, tracking polls are slightly under-measuring Republican support. This may have something to do with the habit of "weighting" the results of the tracking polls, because public opinion polls today rarely produce representative samples. Instead, it becomes necessary to adjust the data to compensate for the over- and under-measuring of different groups that compose the actual electorate. While the polls themselves, and their questions, are down to a science, the weighting cannot be said to be the same. The prediction of who will actually turn out to vote is largely a guessing game, frequently based on the turnout in the last election (*ibid*). This weighting process failed to produce accurate results in 2014 and again in 2016—the former in Kansas, the latter nationwide, more specifically in key battleground states.

Another possibility is that voters are not telling the truth to pollsters about their intentions. Academics call this *social desirability bias*, and one prominent example is called the *Bradley Effect*. The latter is named for Tom Bradley, who was the first highly competitive African American candidate to seek the governorship of California in 1982. Going into the election, polls predicted a win for Bradley. However, in the end, Bradley lost. The conventional wisdom that year was that voters did not want to admit to pollsters that they were not going to vote for Bradley because of his race.

Social desirability bias can occur even in elections where race is not a factor. Was it present in Kansas polling in 2014? With so many people in the chattering class critical of Brownback, many making fun of him, and relentless media coverage of the budget woes, perhaps Brownback supporters played their cards close to their vests. While most were honest, perhaps a thin sliver of Brownback supporters were not forthcoming with pollsters. However, inaccurate weighting remains the most plausible explanation for the polling errors.

In addition, another phenomenon, which is evident in the polling data, could explain the results: the undecideds. Going into the election, there was still a small but significant number of voters who were undecided. These voters appear to have broken heavily toward Brownback and Roberts. Perhaps these voters were undecided because they were not excited about Brownback or Roberts. However, this is Kansas, and many of those voters were probably Republicans or Independents leaning Republican, which means they often vote like Republicans. While not enthusiastic about the Republican candidates this year, they ultimately broke in their favor. Neither Davis nor Orman offered a sufficiently compelling case for crossing party lines.

Also on the ballot that year was Kansas' controversial Secretary of State, Kris Kobach, an outspoken Secretary who transformed a workhorse state office into a platform for anti-immigration policies, claiming that widespread voter fraud was sabotaging Kansas elections. Kobach argued that undocumented immigrants were voting in Kansas elections, undermining democracy. Critics (including the coauthor of this chapter) were not impressed (Smith 2014). In fact, little empirical evidence exists which indicates that voter fraud is widespread in the modern-day United States, and even less that indicates that undocumented immigrants are voting in U.S. elections. This includes Kansas elections. Still, Kobach secured from the Kansas Legislature a law, unseen in any other state, giving the Secretary of State the power to prosecute voter fraud. However, he had prosecuted no undocumented immigrants for voter fraud at this point—only a handful of people who registered and voted in two states. Some of these people were Republicans, and all of them claimed that it was a good faith mistake. They believed that they had a right to vote in local elections in places where they owned property, and they did not vote in federal elections in the two different states.

In 2014, Kobach easily beat Jean Schodorf, a former moderate Republican state senator from Wichita who switched parties to challenge him as a Democrat. Despite Kobach's highly controversial behavior, Schodorf's campaign failed to get off the ground, perhaps because Democrats were more focused on the Davis and Orman campaigns. Schodorf struggled with fundraising and name recognition, and Kobach won reelection easily. It may have also been puzzling to voters that Schodorf, who made her opposition to the SAFE Act the centerpiece of her campaign, had in fact voted for the law's passage when she was a state senator. Kobach was quick to point this out. Schodorf claimed when she cast that vote, she did not expect Kobach to implement the law so aggressively, but that argument just did not catch fire with voters.

RIGGED? DISAPPOINTED AND SEARCHING FOR EXPLANATIONS

Devastated by the unexpected defeats, Democrats and their supporters began reaching for explanations. Some of them suggested malfeasance. In particular, allegations centered on two themes: First, that Kansas' restrictive voting laws had suppressed the Democrats' vote totals, and second, that the state's electronic voting machines were "rigged." Neither argument held up to strict scrutiny, but both did raise serious concerns.

First was the voter-suppression argument. Kobach claimed he had to have the tools to prosecute because of undocumented immigrants sabotaging Kansas elections. He would later prosecute two undocumented immigrants for voter fraud—a very small number. On the other hand, Kobach's critics also exaggerated. In the 2018 *Fish v Kobach* ruling, the U.S. District Court for Kansas found that the Secure and Fair Elections Act led to the removal of more than 30,000 voters from the rolls. The SAFE Act was championed by Kobach and passed in 2011. However, the number of voters whose registrations were not completed due to the law is not a sufficient explanation for the victory of Brownback and Roberts over Davis and Orman. There were not enough votes involved to have flipped the election, particularly because many of the voters removed from the rolls probably would not have voted in a midterm election, when there were no presidential candidates on the ballot.

One other fascinating explanation for the vote totals in 2014 emerged from a Wichita statistician named Beth Clarkson, who was alarmed that Kansas, like many states, had adopted all-electronic voting machines in many counties (Hegeman 2014). This happened as part of the modernization of election equipment after the Help America Vote Act (HAVA) passed in 2003. HAVA came about after decrepit elections equipment in certain counties was blamed, in part, for the debacle of the 2000 presidential election in Florida and the 2000 U.S. Senate election in Missouri. However, even early on, Democrats frequently raised concerns about the electronic voting machines adopted in certain states that did not leave a paper trail, or a way to hand-verify the count. Some Democrats even alleged that these were a factor in the 2004 presidential election, when George W. Bush beat John Kerry, with the closest vote coming in the swing state of Ohio. Several Ohio counties had adopted no-paper-trail, electronic voting machines, some of which were made by companies with ties to the Republican Party.

In Kansas, several counties had also adopted these paperless electronic machines. These included Sedgwick county, location of Wichita. Clarkson produced statistical analyses showing that the vote totals in counties with electronic voting machines appeared to have anomalies compared to the vote totals in counties or precincts using machines that left a paper trail. In essence, Clarkson was arguing that the Kansas' electronic voting machines were skewing vote totals to help Republicans, by not reporting the results accurately. She got no help from Kobach's office, despite her request for data to check her conclusions.

Subsequent re-analyses of Clarkson's findings indicated that many of the changes and differences she observed were also within statistical margins of error. No definitive conclusions could be drawn holding that the machines were "rigged" and that that was the reason for Brownback's and Roberts' reelection victories. However, it is indicative of the mood of skepticism toward Kansas' Republicans by their critics, many of whom were shocked that Roberts and Brownback were in fact reelected. In particular, many Democrats and their supporters were trying to reconcile the polling numbers, which looked so promising, with the actual election results. In 2017 and 2018, evidence would surface that many states' electronic voting machines were vulnerable to hacking and may have been targeted by hackers with ties to Russia.

ELECTION AFTERMATH

A year after the election, loans from Lieutenant Governor Colyer to Governor Brownback again stirred up controversy when the Associated Press revealed that Brownback's campaign spent more than $167,000 in legal fees in 2015 when a federal grand jury was investigating loans to the governor's reelection (Hegeman 2016). No charges were filed. Colyer had made his first $500,000 loan on December 31, 2013, the last day covered by a finance report due in early January 2014, and that loan was repaid on Jan. 2, 2014. Colyer made a second $500,000 loan on July 23, 2014, the second-to-last day covered by a finance report. The loan was repaid two days later. The third $500,000 loan from Colyer was made on August 13, 2014, and a campaign finance disclosure filed in January 2015 indicated that $400,000 of that loan was repaid on November 21, 2014.

Outside observers, including the authors, view the loans as an indicator that the Brownback campaign was concerned that they had not raised more money and, in a Republican state, did not want the voting public to see that the Democratic candidate was able to raise more money than their candidate.

During the campaign, Governor Brownback had proclaimed many times, "the sun is shining in Kansas." Shawn Sullivan, the governor's budget director, reflected the governor's unwavering optimism and resoluteness when he said that the mounting deficit was "certainly manageable through good fiscal governance." However, revenue reports indicated there were clouds on the horizon. According to former Kansas Budget Director Duane Goossen, Kansas was in serious financial trouble (Goossen 2014b).

The legislature approved $6.325 billion in expenses for FY 2015, and the state began the 2015 fiscal year with a reserve of $380 million. Even with that reserve, the state had to collect $5.945 billion just to balance the budget. However, FY 2014 state revenue totaled $5.653 billion; if FY 2015 revenue were to equal FY 2014 revenue, the state still would need to cut expenses by $292 million. If the trend continued, it was clear that the state income was below estimate and would soon burn through the $380 million balance on hand at the beginning of the fiscal year, and the state would start running a deficit, which is not permitted by the Kansas Constitution. That would mean that budget cuts would be required. State services—especially education, which accounted for about half of state expenditures—would face cuts in the next legislative session.

Implementation of the "great experiment," that included the large 2012 and 2013 tax cuts, was with the expectation that the economy would get a boost—a boost that was not evident by the end of 2014. Whether the experiment was working had yet to be determined

CHAPTER SUMMARY

Sam Brownback had begun implementation of his "great experiment" in 2012 with major tax cuts intended to give the Kansas economy "a shot of adrenalin." Reelection was essential to continue implementation of his plan. Early in the campaign a number of Republican leaders expressed their concern for Brownback's leadership and backed Democrat Paul Davis. Both Brownback and Davis focused the campaign for governor on Brownback's tax cuts to stimulate the economy. After a hard-fought campaign, Brownback won a narrow victory in the election that brought a solid majority of his Republican Party to the House of Representatives and to the cabinet. The right people were in place for continued implementation of the Brownback agenda, but revenue trends suggested financial trouble ahead for Kansas.

REFERENCES

Associated Press. 2014. "Groups Spent Nearly $17M on Kansas Senate Race." *Associated Press State Wire, Kansas*, November 7.

Campaign Finance Institute. 2019. "Kansas 2014 Elections." *FollowTheMoney.org*. https://www.followthemoney.org/tools/election-overview?s=KS&y=2014.

Carpenter, Tim. 2014a. "Brownback Formally Steps into Re-Election Ring." *Topeka Capital-Journal*, May 15.

Carpenter, Tim. 2014b. "More Than 100 GOP Politicians Endorse Democrat Davis for Governor." *Topeka Capital-Journal*, July 15.

Carpenter, Tim. 2014c. "It's Nearly Over: Kansas Candidates Racing to Finish." *Topeka Capital-Journal,* November 3.

Clarkson, Beth. 2017. "Testimony for the Oct 27th Meeting of the Joint Committee on Ethics and Election." October 25. http://showmethevotes.org/2017/10/25/testimony-for-the-oct-27th-meeting-of-the-joint-committee-on-ethics-and-election.

Cooper, Brad. 2014. "Kansas Tax Revenues Fall While Others States See Rise." *Kansas City Star*, May 10.

Flentje, Ed. 2018. Interview by Michael A. Smith, May 31.

Goossen, Duane. 2014a. "Don't Believe the Revenue Estimates—Kansas' Budget Has Already Gone Off the Fiscal Cliff." *The Kansas Budget Blog*, July 22. http://www.kansasbudget.com/2014/07.

Goossen, Duane. 2014b. "Now It's Official: The Kansas Budget is Crashing." *The Kansas Budget Blog*, November 11. http://www.kansasbudget.com/2014/11.

Grover, Bob. 2014. "Brownback's Fiction: More Money for Education." *The Emporia Gazette,* August 15.

Grover, Bob and Jim Calvert. 2014a. "Davis's Top Priorities: Economy and Schools." *Emporia Gazette*, September 26.

Grover, Bob and Jim Calvert. 2014b. "Davis Discusses Health Care and Leadership." *Emporia Gazette*, October 3.

Hegeman, Roxana. 2014. "Voting Machine Tapes Questioned." *Topeka Capital-Journal,* October 17.

Hegeman, Roxana. 2016. "Sam Brownback's Campaign Spent $167,000 in Legal Fees." *Topeka Capital Journal,* January 8.

Helling, Dave and Brad Cooper. 2014. "Kansas Candidate's Loan Ignites Debate." *Kansas City Star*, January 20.

Kansas State Fair Debate. 2014. "Audio Recording by Bob Grover from a Live Radio Broadcast." September 6.

Marso, Andy. 2014. "Expert Forecast: Kansas Will Be in the Red Within a Year Without Changes." *Topeka Capital-Journal*, June 3.

Orman, Greg. 2016. *A Declaration of Independents*. Austin, TX: Greenleaf Book Group.

Rackaway, Chapman. 2015. "Insight Kansas: Don't Call It A Comeback?" *Hays Post,* October 23.

Roy, Bill. 2014. "Davis, Winn Emerge as Winners in Tuesday's Primary." *Wichita Business Journal*, August 6. https://www.bizjournals.com/wichita/blog/2014/08/davis-winn-emerge-as-winners-in-tuesday-s-primary.html.

Shorman, Jonathan. 2014. "Christie Once Again Campaigns for Brownback." *Topeka Capital-Journal*, October 20.

Smith, Michael A. 2017. "Polling for the 2016 Presidential Election: What Went Wrong." *Midwest Political Science Association Blog*, January 11. https://blog.mpsanet.org/2017/01/11/polling-for-the-2016-presidential-election.

Chapter 7

Brownback's Second Term

End of the Experiment

CHAPTER OVERVIEW

Brownback opened his second term announcing "full steam ahead." Saying "it has not been easy," he announced his continued support for the Experiment and began attacking President Obama. His supporter, House Speaker Ray Merrick, chimed in by attacking public workers and even the revenue estimates themselves, while Senate president Susan Wagle attempted to be the conciliator.

In 2015, the Legislature voted to end the school base funding formula and replace it with two-year block grants. The formula was reinstated in 2017. Also in 2015, the Legislature had its longest session in Kansas history, as debate raged over various tax proposals, culminating in a sales tax increase. However, in 2016, with more short-term budget fixes, court rulings on school funding, and bad news about the budget, voters had enough. Moderates and Democrats won more than fifteen house and senate seats from Brownback supporters.

In 2017, the new Moderate-Democrat coalition brushed aside Brownback's proposals and, after a long, drawn-out process, voted to close the LLC exemption and add a third tax bracket. Brownback was not a player in this process, providing only vetoes, which were overridden at the last minute when several house members and one senator changed their votes. Even afterward, the Kansas Supreme Court continued to rule that the school funding was unconstitutional and set future court dates for the *Gannon* case.

LAFFER CURVE OR STARVE THE BEAST?

Brownback's rhetoric about the "Glide Path to Zero" was always relentlessly optimistic, exemplified by his "Sun is Shining in Kansas" television ad in

2014. Yet, the hopeful Laffer Curve—the argument that tax cuts self-fund by stimulating enough economic growth to self-fund by broadening the tax base—is only one of two divergent arguments made by political conservatives in favor of tax cuts (see chapter 4). The other is usually called "Starve the Beast." Anti-tax activist Grover Norquist once said, "I don't want to abolish government. I simply want to reduce it to the size where I can drag it into the bathroom and drown it in the bathtub" (Spross 2017).

As detailed by right-leaning *National Review* writer Kevin D. Williamson, Starve the Beast holds that tax cuts will, in fact, result in diminishing revenues, forcing government to stop or even reverse its growth. Writing specifically about Kansas, Williamson quotes state representative Owen Donohoe, who called the 2012 tax cut "the greatest thing that's ever happened to Kansas" because it would "force us to be more efficient." A bona fide conservative himself, Williamson notes that the in Kansas, as in other states, the budget consists mostly of education funding, roads, employee compensation, and local aid. He dismisses Donohoe's views as "delusional." Williamson continues, "We are not going to balance the federal budget without cutting Social Security and other popular entitlements as well as the military, and Kansas is not going to bring its spending down to match a lower revenue line without touching education and the roads. It isn't going to happen" (Williamson 2016).

In Kansas, Williamson's analysis proved remarkably accurate. The Legislature cut government where they could, for example, severely short-staffing the state's prisons. But other attempts to keep the state solvent included borrowing that downgraded the state's bond rating, draining the state's highway trust fund, block-granting the base state aid formula for schools, and even delaying pension contributions into the next year. On the tax side, a marathon session of the Legislature in 2015 resulted in a sales tax increase, but that was only enough to partially offset the revenue lost from the 2012 income tax cuts.

What follows is the rest of the story.

2015: THINGS BEGIN TO FALL APART

Full Steam Ahead?

Shortly after the 2014 election, an AP Wire story announced, "Brownback wins despite muted support for tax plan" (Hanna 2014). The story cited a poll by Edison Research in which roughly half of those surveyed said that Brownback's tax cut had benefitted the state, but two in five said that it had hurt. The story also noted the governor's narrow reelection victory.

On the other hand, statehouse returns told a different story. Brownback became one of only two Republican Kansas governors to win reelection during the past 50 years (Wagoner 2014) and Republicans held their supermajorities in the Legislature. Within the House and Senate GOP caucuses, conservatives kept their majorities within the party.

Brownback wasted no time announcing full steam ahead. On election night, he said, "We made bold moves in the state of Kansas and sometimes tough moves to get our state growing again. It has not been easy, but doing the right thing rarely is" (ibid.).

Unfortunately for the governor, revenue estimates, court rulings, and other news did not share his optimism. The budget forecast released just after the election indicated that the state needed to cut $279 million from its current year's budget just to finish with a zero balance (Lowry 2014). A three-judge panel in Shawnee County (Topeka) green-lighted a new lawsuit on school finance—one which could result in more money, anywhere from $450 million to $1.4 billion, being allocated to base per-pupil state aid. The panel also chided the state for their increasing reliance on Local Option Budgets (LOB)—essentially, local property taxes—to cover school finances. The increased reliance on LOB signaled a return to the days before the base state aid formula passed in the early 1990s. Back then, the wide variation in property assessments from one school district to another led to huge disparities in school funding, which the formula was intended to fix. The judges worried that the state was slipping back toward this inequality (ibid.).

There was also good news, and the governor and his allies were quick to seize upon it. However, critics often chimed in to temper. For example, November revenue receipts beat estimates by $3.1 million (Shorman 2014), but this came after a $23 million shortfall in October. Federal figures showed a gain of 8,400 jobs in October—but Abouhalkah (2014) noted that this rate of job growth (2.4 percent) trailed all of Kansas' neighbors except Nebraska.

Finally, the Administration was excited about a new federal report that, they claimed, showed a 2 percent drop in poverty statewide. However, critics forced a retraction, showing that the Department of Children and Families had misread the federal report. Poverty in Kansas had in fact grown slightly (Editors 2014). They also noted high poverty rates among Kansas children and rebutted Brownback's claims that the data showed success moving people from welfare to work. Welfare rolls had indeed been cut by about half, but this was due to tightened eligibility, not necessarily to the recipients finding jobs (ibid.) All of Brownback's good news, it seemed, got tempered by critics. The "new normal" trends reinserted themselves in December, when revenues came in $15 million below estimates (Shorman 2014a).

In his 2015 State of the State Address, Brownback took aim directly at the school funding formula, giving no ground and initiating a new line of attack.

He proposed a simpler formula with about a dozen weighting factors—far fewer than the existing system. According to the governor and his allies, the problem with the schools was not inequality of funding, but wasteful spending on excessive administration. "For decades now," the governor said, "Kansas has struggled under a school finance formula which is designed not to be understood, to frustrate efforts at accountability and efficiency, a formula designed to lock in automatic, massive increases in spending unrelated to actual student populations or improved student achievement" (Lowry and Cooper 2015).

The governor then took aim at the courts themselves, calling for an end to the merit system, or Missouri Nonpartisan Court Plan. Before his reelection, he successfully convinced legislators to change the Kansas Court of Appeals selection process. The primary goal was to eliminate the commission that recommends three nominees to the governor to fill vacant judicial positions. Under the new system, the list was eliminated, and the governor was now able to submit the name of any nominee he chose. With state senate approval, the nominee would be confirmed. The periodic retention elections used earlier would be maintained. In a move that some observers took as a direct swipe at the state supreme court, Brownback proposed to expand this new system beyond appellate courts.

In short, the governor's tone was highly confrontational, particularly regarding the school funding issue and his dispute with the courts.

For their part, Republican legislative leaders took different tacks regarding this combative stance, starting in late 2014. A few weeks before Brownback's address, Senate President Susan Wagle seemed to moderate things a bit, stating that lawmakers have a duty to look at taxes and spending to balance the equation (Lowry 2014). House Speaker Ray Merrick chose instead to take a strong conservative line. Merrick liked to quote Ronald Reagan, stating that the state does not have a revenue problem; it has a spending problem, which one legislator likened to slamming a door that Wagle had left open (ibid.). Far more controversial were his remarks regarding government workers. In a widely quoted gaffe, Merrick told the *Wichita Eagle*, "Government employees produce nothing. They're a net consumer. And you get that cost forever and ever and ever because they're on the (state pension) plan, they're on all the government insurance and everything" (Abouhalkah 2014a).

Editorialists and teachers' organizations (particularly the Kansas National Education Association) seized on these remarks with harsh criticism. A "fire Ray Merrick" petition was even bandied about by teachers, firefighters, and police officers. Merrick walked back the comments shortly afterward, praising the "vital role" that state workers have in the economy, but critics had a new hook to use in attacking the conservatives—and a deepened apprehension about what was to come.

Kicking the Can with Block Grants: The *Gannon* Decision

The Kansas Supreme Court did not rule again on school funding during the 2015 legislative session, so the earlier ruling by a three-judge panel remained the most current material available to the governor and the Legislature to use when writing the budget. While the earlier reading of the decision indicated a wide variation in possible amounts of additional money required, subsequent analyses narrowed the estimate of additional money to between $550 and $770 million (Llopis-Jepsen 2015). Some observers suggested that Brownback's proposed new formula was in fact a strategy to buy time with the courts. Reporter Celia Llopis-Jepsen quoted Rutgers University Professor Bruce Baker, who specializes in school finance. Baker said, "This has been tried in any number of states. Call it a different formula. Call it something structurally completely different, even if it's not. Give it a new name."

According to Baker, as quoted by Llopis-Jepsen, this could be the basis of a legal argument for the court to dismiss a case, due to the fact that the formula being litigated no longer exists.

In the end, the Legislature did choose to end the school funding formula, which had been in effect for nearly a quarter century. They further accepted Brownback's recommendation that the formula be replaced with block grants, at least temporarily. The amount of spending was set based upon the amount that school districts had received the previous year. Controversy erupted immediately, for several reasons. First, while the three-judge panel had called for at least half a million dollars to be put into schools, the governor's proposal actually cut funding by at least $20 million. Second, the governor's proposal re-calculated pension contributions, shifting more of their cost onto the school districts' allocations and reducing funding for other programs. According to Senate Minority Leader Anthony Hensley, once pension changes were accounted, the actual cut to schools was nearly $100 million. Finally, the block grant proposal included no per-pupil formula, thus schools were unable to secure state money to fund increases in student enrollment—and the accompanying costs (ibid.).

In the end, the Legislature chose a combination. On the one hand, they passed the block grants requested by the governor, replacing the old formula. On the other, they sought to appease the courts by at least funding the increases in school funding called for in the previous year's budget. Yet trouble remained. At the end of the regular session, the Legislature passed a budget that called for an overall $400 million of spending increases, mostly in education and social services. However, they did not pass a revenue package to fund it (Hanna 2015). As the "wrap up session" (formerly known as the veto session) began, the stage was set for the Kansas Legislature to hold its longest session in history.

Marathon Session

In the end, the Kansas Legislature voted in 2015 to increase sales taxes. The process to get there featured many twists, turns, false starts, and dead ends.

It started with the governor's budget, which proposed higher alcohol and tobacco taxes, a temporary freeze on the "Glide Path to Zero" (income taxes) and eliminating several income tax deductions. The alcoholic beverage tax would rise from 8 to 12 percent, and the tax on cigarettes from $0.79 to $2.29. The deal was sweetened just slightly by a cut to the lowest income tax bracket. Additional fund sweeps and budget cuts accompanied the proposal.

The alcohol and tobacco vendors were highly critical of the proposed tax hikes on their products, noting that many of their customers were lower-income (Lowry 2015), and Democrats concurred. For their part, the Legislature was unable to pass the tax increases to fund their own budget by the end of regular session. This is common, but the length of the wrap-up session was not. Legislators set a state record, working well into June, considering and rejecting a vast array of revenue options for funding. The possibility of ending the LLC exemption was bandied about again and again, but could never get enough votes to pass, and did not become part of the final deal.

In late April, new revenue estimates doubled the projected revenue shortfall. Now, the legislators needed to find $800 million to fund their budget including the fix for schools. Unable to find a solution in May, legislators entered June facing the possibility of furloughing state workers. Notices went out, but the problem was averted by a last-minute work-around: declaring all state workers "essential" (Associated Press 2015). Still, the budget remained underfunded. House and Senate leaders complained that the governor showed little leadership during this time, leaving Republicans to divide into several different factions, each with their own agenda regarding taxes (Shorman 2015).

National publicity piled on: *Salon,* the *Washington Post, U.S. News & World Report,* and the comic strip *Doonesbury* all highlighted what one called "Political Dysfunction in Oz" (Editors 2015; Llopis-Jepsen 2015a). Still no deal was forthcoming. Besides the division of the GOP into factions and the usual house-senate disagreements, the stalemate was rooted in the hesitation of many Republicans to vote for *any* tax increase, combined with the fact that the Democrats hung tough and voted no on everything. Democratic leaders argued, first, that the problem was created by Republicans and it was their responsibility to fix it, and second, that the taxes under consideration were simultaneously too regressive and insufficient to close the budget gap. The GOP had to find a way to pass the fix without a single Democratic vote.

Finally, in mid-June, legislative leaders cobbled together the minimum number of votes in each house needed to pass a bill raising the sales tax from

6.15 to 6.5 percent (Lowry 2015a). Because Kansas is one of the few states that fully applies the sales tax to groceries, this made the state's grocery tax one of the nation's highest. Proposals for a grocery tax break were considered, but did not make it into the final bill. A fifty cent per pack cigarette tax also passed, along with some business tax changes and the elimination of most itemized income tax deductions. The Legislature also threw in a requirement that local property tax increases get voter approval, a private school scholarship tax credit, and an amnesty program for back taxes (Hanna 2015a). Two concerns remained. Democrats immediately attacked the bill as regressive (Lowry 2015a). Also, the bill raised just under $400 million—less than half the amount needed for the budget, based on revenue estimates.

The marathon session was over. The Kansas Legislature had passed tax increases to partially plug the budget hole, with little help from the governor. Democrats spent the session positioning themselves as critics and pinning the problem on Brownback and his Republican allies, rather than being part of the budget negotiations. Moderate Republicans were restive. The following year, the voters would have their say. First, however, the Legislature would have to throw in the kitchen sink just to get through the next year, then punt to the governor.

2016: VOTERS END THE EXPERIMENT

More Bad News

The year 2016 began with more bad news for the governor. The December 2015 revenue collections fell $27 million below expectation—despite the fact that the expectation had been lowered shortly beforehand (Shorman 2016). Editorialists warned of a crisis in law enforcement: a 16 percent vacancy rate among correctional staff, turnover nearing 30 percent, and a shortage in the Highway Patrol staffing as well. The problem stemmed from low pay, and the money was not available to match the pay in other area states like Iowa and Colorado, which paid these workers about $10,000 more annually (Eveld 2016). The 2015 tax amnesty program netted $23 million, falling $7 million short of expectation (Shorman 2016b). Finally, the Kansas Supreme Court had set a June 30 deadline to fix—or at least show progress in—school funding (Shorman 2016b).

Whose Fault? The Governor and Allies Respond

With the current year's budget shortfall estimated at $19 million, the governor and his conservative allies developed a number of interesting responses to the dire situation. Conservative responses could be grouped by the state's three GOP leaders. According to Senate President Wagle, the problem was an international recession that affected oil, gas, and agricultural commodity prices. According to Brownback himself, the real problem was not the state budget at all; it was President Obama and interest groups with which he was allied—particularly Planned Parenthood. Finally, Speaker Merrick, something of a loose cannon, tried attacking the revenue estimates themselves.

Wagle was the first to speak, telling fellow senators, "We are in this situation because we are in an international recession" (Shorman 2016c). Later that year, Brownback and allies would frequently invoke the resource and commodity prices to explain the budget troubles. Goossen, now a senior fellow at the Kansas Center for Economic Growth, continued to disagree (ibid.), but by April, the governor had adopted this line of attack, focusing particularly on commodity prices (Lowry 2016).

Brownback took a different tack than Wagle when giving his State of the State Address. The governor pivoted away from budget questions entirely and focused his criticism on President Obama. Brownback invoked a fear that Obama might close the Guantanamo Bay detention facility, that "terrorists" (terrorism suspects and material witnesses awaiting trial) could be transferred to Fort Leavenworth. He also attacked Planned Parenthood, raising a criticism circulating among the organization's critics that they were "trafficking in baby body parts," a charge that most other observers considered discredited. Brownback renewed his call to change judge selection—a proposal that went nowhere in 2015—and blamed the Affordable Care Act (ACA—"Obamacare") for rising rural healthcare costs. He also defended the KanCare privatization model and said it was a better alternative to the ACA (ibid.).

In short, Brownback's strategy that year was to attack President Obama and Planned Parenthood, while doubling down on KanCare and his attempts to change judge selection. Few, if any solutions to the budget shortfalls were mentioned.

The third line of rebuttal did not emerge until April. It came from Speaker Merrick, and featured his typical outspokenness. Merrick decided to attack the budget estimates themselves, arguing that the budget should be based only on receipts and not on the Consensus Revenue Estimates that the state had used for many years. Merrick said on a podcast, "I've been in the Legislature 17 years . . . I never, never knew how you could run governments on estimates. Right? The real number, we're at $53 million ahead of a year ago. To me, that's the real number. It's not six guys sitting around in a room doing an estimate" (Shorman 2016d). The Speaker also acknowledged that the process was unlikely to change. Critics were quick to point out that the estimates were, if anything, overly optimistic most months, and that the $53 million he cited included increases in insurance premiums (ibid.).

Backlash

Interest groups representing those affected by the cuts became emboldened in 2016, starting with a billboard campaign by highway contractors. Under the message "Highway Robbery" and a stock photo of an archetypical bandit with a mask, stocking cap, and gun, the billboards protested transfer of more than $300 million annually ("more than $1 million per day," according to the message) from the highway fund into general revenues. Critics also protested a proposal for "tobacco securitization"—essentially, selling off the right to collect on future settlements from the tobacco lawsuits of the late 1990s and early 2000s. The money was being deposited into a children's health trust fund. The governor promised to fund the program from general revenues instead—but only for one year (Lowry 2016a). Even Attorney General Derek Schmidt, a Republican who normally kept a low profile, got into the fray when he told an agricultural group that "Actually, if you read the letter of the law in the Kansas Constitution, it doesn't say there has to be a balanced budget," inviting further controversy. Schmidt claimed that the state constitution required only "suitable provision," which could include issuing bonds (Griekspoor 2016). Finally, unions representing law enforcement officers called further attention to the prison and Highway Patrol staffing shortfall.

The Kitchen Sink

The final budget that passed included many of the controversial ideas above, and more. Hoping to satisfy the courts as June 30 approached, $2 million was transferred from an extraordinary needs fund to education, and the Local Option Budget was tweaked, with many districts gaining money and those that would have lost money protected by a special hold-harmless clause (Shorman 2016e). A $17 million increase was also allocated for the state's mental hospitals in Larned and Osawatomie. The latter had lost its federal certification due to short staffing and other problems (Lowry 2016b).

To fund this budget, the Legislature threw in the kitchen sink—and then punted to the governor. April contribution to the state employees' pension fund was delayed, shifting nearly $100 million to the next fiscal year, including an 8 percent surcharge for paying late (Eveld 2016a). The highway cuts started hitting home. Unlike previous years, when KDOT always promised to complete existing projects, they now stated that while this was still the case, they would also delay 25 large highway projects that had been scheduled to start soon (Editors 2016). The state Bioscience Authority was sold, netting $25 million. The Legislature called for step therapy for Medicaid recipients, which essentially means trying the least expensive treatment first and then working up based on cost, which was estimated to save $11 million (Lowry 2016b).

Even with these cuts, the bill, passed by the minimum number of votes needed in the House and by only two to spare in the Senate, did not balance the budget. Legislators called upon the governor to make the rest of the cuts using his discretionary authority (ibid.). Speculation abounded—for example, many expected him to cut funding for universities—but in the end, the Legislature simply left the budget unbalanced and handed it back to the governor to make the rest of the cuts.

That fall, the voters would have their say.

The 2016 Elections: End of an Era

The bad budget news kept on coming. There was no clear resolution to the education funding dilemma in sight—the Legislature kept sweeping in what they thought was the minimum amount of money needed to keep the courts from closing the schools. In the August primaries, moderate Republicans, running as a ticket on statewide issues, hammered Brownback and his allies on the budget and school funding (Hanna 2016). This strategy was particularly effective in Johnson County. First, the county was known for having good schools, a major draw for families who lived there. Second, the area was more densely populated than rural Kansas, so many voters did not know which House or Senate District was the one in which they lived—having the moderates together on a ticket helped resolve this confusion. Third, active groups such as the Mainstream Coalition were heavily involved in phone banking and door knocking to promote the ticket. One Johnson County yard sign featured the message, "Stop Brownback" together with a Republican elephant. The moderates were back.

While Johnson County was the epicenter, moderates pounced in other areas of the state as well. In Hutchinson, for example, Senate Majority Leader Terry Bruce faced a tough challenge from Ed Berger, a former community college president well positioned to run on education.

In the end, it was no contest. Bruce lost, as did 13 other conservative incumbents. Five house members and two senators defeated hailed from Johnson County. All were Brownback allies. The rest—Bruce, two more senators, and three more house members—came from around the state. Moderates were less successful in the Wichita area—but Democrats were ready to mount the mop-up operation.

In the fall, Democrats ran on similar themes as had the moderates in the summer. However, they also stressed one point the moderates had overlooked—tax fairness. They called attention to the fact that the substitution of sales tax revenue (particularly on groceries) for income tax revenue made the system more regressive. Like the moderates, they also hammered on the budget mess and the school funding shortfall.

The Democrats did particularly well in and around Wichita, winning against conservatives that the moderates had not been able to unseat—a sort of mop-up operation (Lowry and Lefler 2016). One seat flipped the other direction, as the strongly conservative Brenda Landwehr regained her old house seat, but overall, the Democrats' mop-up activities set the stage for a Moderate-Republican coalition to stop the "glide path" and perhaps even reverse Brownback's Great Experiment.

2017: THE KANSAS LEGISLATURE ENDS THE EXPERIMENT

More Bad News

The next year began with more bad news. While revenue for December 2016 exceeded estimates, the state still faced a $342 million shortfall. The governor announced he would not release a plan until the Legislature was back in session (Woodall 2017). Brownback also announced that he wanted restrictive new limits on public welfare eligibility and expressed his hope these would gain national publicity (Shorman 2017). The previous year, the governor had signed a bill lowering the benefit limit for Temporary Assistance to Needy Families to 24 calendar months instead of 36, and to 36 months over a recipient's lifetime, instead of 48. The bill also put a host of restrictions on how the money could be used (ibid.).

Also on the agenda was school funding. When the previous Legislature had ended the base funding formula and enacted block grants in 2015, they had set the grants to be temporary. They were set to expire at the end of 2017. The clock was ticking, and more court rulings loomed as well (Shorman 2017a). Speaking of the Kansas courts—they, too, faced funding shortfalls. Chief Justice Lawton Nuss warned that the court system might face furloughs if their own budget shortfall was not fixed (Associated Press 2017).

The Hard Work Begins

Early efforts to close the budget shortfall focused on the LLC exemption, which many of the newly elected moderates and Democrats viewed as a loophole and sought to close (Hanna 2017). Many had even said so while seeking office. However, the governor remained opposed, arguing that new jobs were coming and saying, "I'd hate to see us walking away from something that's really taking off" (ibid.). The estimate was that closing the exemption would raise $260 million a year. Notable controversy surrounded a proposal to make the tax reinstatement retroactive to the beginning of the year (Shorman 2017b).

Reelected as Senate President, Wagle signaled willingness to compromise, saying she would support "permanent solutions" to the budget problems and criticizing proposed one-time fixes such as liquidating another state fund (Associated Press 2017). The House elected a conservative-moderate team as their new leaders: Conservative Rob Rykman, Jr. of Olathe was joined by moderate Don Hineman of Dighton. House committee chairs represented both moderate and conservative factions—a sharp break from the conservative dominance of the last house session (ibid.). For their part, Democrats elected Wichita's Jim Ward as their Minority Leader. Ward was known for being more fiery than outgoing leader Tom Burroughs of Kansas City.

In the State of the State Address, Brownback called for "modest, targeted" taxes to fill the shortfall, drawing further criticism (Hanna 2017a). He also called for a new school funding formula, merit pay for teachers, startup money for a new private osteopathy school, a bachelor's degree program that costs only $15,000 total, and a dental school at the University of Kansas Medical Center. Reactions to the State of the State were muted (Woodall 2017a).

The governor's proposed budget included tobacco taxes, reduced pension contributions, and liquidating a state stabilization fund. He also proposed a "passive income" tax on silent business partners, and an increase in the for-profit business filing fee (Carpenter 2017). Wasting no words, Democratic Rep. Tom Sawyer of Wichita called the proposal "a pile of garbage" (Hanna 2017b). In general, legislators generally brushed aside Brownback's proposals and wrote their own budget that year, and he did not appear to be a major player. Critics later estimated that the proposed pension changes would cost the state an additional $6.5 million in the long term (Lowry 2017). Brownback later signaled that he would support a "partial repeal" of the LLC exemption (Shorman 2017c).

Still more bad news came when an audit of KanCare—the governor's privatized approach to Medicaid—found it to be "substantially out of compliance" with U.S. law, putting funding at risk (Shorman 2017d). Concerns included "beneficiaries' receipt of services necessary to stay in the community, beneficiaries' ability to access needed care, and the state's ability to ensure the health and welfare of beneficiaries" (ibid.).

A mid-year estimate found that if the budget were balanced without new taxes, a 6.9 percent across-the-board reduction in state spending would be required, hitting school funding with particular force (Carpenter 2017a). The Supreme Court followed up with another ruling in March, unanimously finding current funding to be inadequate (Shorman 2017e).

A Long, Drawn-Out Ending

In the end, the Legislature overrode Brownback's veto and reinstated the LLC taxes and a third income tax bracket, while failing to override his veto of Medicaid expansion. The final bill raised income taxes by $1.2 billion over the next two years. With furloughs looming again, the bill passed in June—long after the Legislature would have normally adjourned—by thin margins to override the veto (Carpenter 2017b). The Senate passed it with the minimum two-thirds majority needed, while the House topped its minimum by four votes. More than a dozen legislators who had previously backed the governor, mostly House members, switched their votes to support the override.

The governor's proposals, including tobacco taxes, reduced pension contributions, and fund liquidation, were not included in the final bill. *The Atlantic* gave the vote national publicity, announcing "The Death of Kansas' Conservative Experiment" (Berman 2017). One legislator, Democrat Patsy Terrell of Hutchinson, collapsed and died in her hotel room shortly after casting her vote to override the veto (Hrenchir 2017). She had been elected in 2016 on an anti-Brownback platform.

The Experiment was over, but the hard decisions were not. In October, the Kansas Supreme Court ruled that the state's school funding was still out of balance (Woodall 2017b).

CHAPTER SUMMARY

Brownback began his second term by announcing his continued support for the Great Experiment, and he began attacking President Obama and his programs, apparently searching for reasons his plan was not stimulating the state's economy and providing revenue for the state. In 2015, the Legislature voted to end the school base funding formula, but it was reinstated in 2017. Also in 2015, the Legislature passed a sales tax increase to address the declining revenue. In 2016, with more short-term budget fixes and continued bad news about the budget, voters elected moderates and Democrats to more than 15 house and senate seats, defeating Brownback supporters.

In 2017, the moderate-Democratic coalition voted to close the LLC exemption and add a third tax bracket. Brownback's vetoes were overridden, and the Great Experiment was nearing an end.

REFERENCES

Abouhalkah, Yael T. 2014. "Stunning New Surge of Jobs in Kansas Will Put Big Smile on Sam Brownback's Face." *Kansas City Star*, November 21.

Abouhalkah, Yael T. 2014a. "Ignore Ray Merrick's Foolish Comments; Government Workers in Kansas Are Not Parasites." *Kansas City Star*, November 19.

Associated Press. 2015. "Kansas Governor to Sign a Bill Aimed at Averting Furloughs." June 6.

Associated Press. 2017. "The Latest: Top Kansas Lawmaker Wants 'Permanent' Budget Fix." January 9.

Carpenter, Tim. 2017. "Brownback's Budget Raises Taxes, Alters Pension and Medicaid Funding." *Topeka Capital-Journal*, January 11.

Carpenter, Tim. 2017a. "Fact Meter: Brownback, Sullivan 'Structurally Balanced' Budget Claims Fall Short." *Topeka Capital-Journal,* January 22.

Carpenter, Tim. 2017b. "Senate, House Narrowly Override Gov. Sam Brownback's Veto of $1.2 Billion Tax Bill." *Topeka Capital-Journal*, June 6.

Editors. 2014. "Brownback Administration Can't Sugarcoat Kansas Poverty Count." *Kansas City Star*, November 17.

Editors. 2015. "'Dysfunction in Oz': National News Outlets Paint Bleak Picture of Kansas." *Topeka Capital-Journal*, June 11.

Editors. 2016. "Highway Project Delays Could Cause Safety Issues." *Associated Press*, April 25.

Eveld, Edward M. 2016. "Kansas Is Short on Prison Guards, Highway Patrol Troopers Amid Budget Woes." *Kansas City Star*, January 3.

Eveld, Edward M. 2016a. "Kansas Delays Contribution to State Employee Pension System." *Kansas City Star*, April 8.

Griekspoor, P. J. 2016. "Kansas Is Not Required to Balance Its Budget?" *Wichita Eagle*, April 2.

Hanna, John. 2014. "Brownback Wins Despite Muted Support For Tax Plan." *Associated Press*, November 5.

Hanna, John. 2015. "Kansas Budget Chief Lays Out Possible Cuts." *Associated Press*, June 9.

Hanna, John. 2015a. "Kansas Lawmakers' Tax Plan Makes Numerous Policy Changes." *Associated Press*, June 13.

Hanna, John. 2016. "GOP Moderates Make Kansas Primary about Schools, Budget Woes." *Associated Press*, August 2.

Hanna, John. 2017. "Kansas Governor, Lawmakers at Odds over Repealing Tax Break." *Associated Press*, January 7.

Hanna, John. 2017a. "Kansas Governor to Seek 'Modest' Tax Increases to Fix Budget." *Associated Press*, January 10.

Hanna, John. 2017b. "Kansas Governor's Budget Fix: Higher Taxes, Tobacco Funds." *Associated Press*, January 11.

Hrenchir, Tim. 2017. "County Coroner: Rep. Patsy Terrell's Death Was Due to Natural Causes." *Topeka Capital-Journal*, June 15.

Llopis-Jepsen, Celia. 2015. "Brownback K-12 Plan Prompts Questions of Court Maneuver." *Topeka Capital-Journal,* January 19.

Llopis-Jepsen, Celia. 2015a. "Comic Strip Doonesbury Tackles Kansas School Funding and Budget Deficits." *Topeka Capital-Journal*, June 7.

Lowry, Bryan. 2014. "Kansas Lawmakers Divide into Two Camps on How to Plug $1 Billion Budget Hole." *Wichita Eagle,* November 15.

Lowry, Bryan. 2015. "Brownback Seeks To Raise Kansas Tobacco And Liquor Taxes, Scale Back Deductions." *Kansas City Star,* January 16.

Lowry, Bryan. 2015a. "Tax Plan Passes Kansas House and Senate, Brownback Set to Sign." *Kansas City Star,* June 12.

Lowry, Bryan. 2016. "Brownback Blames Budget Shortfall on Dropping Commodity Prices, Balks at Tax Increase." *Kansas City Star,* April 22.

Lowry, Bryan. 2016a. "'Tobacco Securitization' And What It Would Mean For Kansas." *Wichita Eagle,* April 22.

Lowry, Bryan. 2016b. "Kansas Lawmakers Narrowly Pass Budget Fix, Adjourn." *Wichita Eagle,* May 1.

Lowry, Bryan. 2017. "Long-term Pension Costs in Kansas Would Rise by $6 Billion under Brownback Plan." *Kansas City Star,* January 12.

Lowry, Bryan and Brad Cooper. 2015. "Gov. Sam Brownback, Wrestling with Budget Shortages, Says Kansas Is Headed in the Right Direction." *Kansas City Star,* January 15.

Lowry, Bryan and Dion Lefler. 2016. "Democrats Make Gains in Kansas Legislature." *Wichita Eagle,* November 8.

Shorman, Jonathan. 2014. "November Revenue Beats Estimate by $3.1 Million." *Topeka Capital-Journal,* November 26.

Shorman, Jonathan. 2014a. "Brownback to Cut State Agency Spending by 4 Percent in Response to Revenue Shortfall." *Topeka Capital-Journal,* December 9.

Shorman, Jonathan. 2015. "Analysis: Why Lawmakers Reached Day 107." *Topeka Capital-Journal,* June 6.

Shorman, Jonathan. 2016. "Kansas Revenue Plunged $27 Million below Expectations in December." *Topeka Capital-Journal,* January 4.

Shorman, Jonathan. 2016a. "Kansas Tax Amnesty Snagged $23M, $7M Less than Expected." *Topeka Capital-Journal,* January 7.

Shorman, Jonathan. 2016b. "Sam Brownback Signs Kansas School Finance Legislation Responding to Court Order." *Topeka Capital-Journal,* April 7.

Shorman, Jonathan. 2016c. "Faced with Budget Shortfall, Republicans Point to Global Economic Troubles as Session Begins." *Topeka Capital-Journal,* January 11.

Shorman, Jonathan. 2016d. "House Speaker Ray Merrick Expresses Frustration with Estimate-Based Budgeting." *Topeka Capital-Journal,* April 12.

Shorman, Jonathan. 2016e. "Sam Brownback Signs Kansas School Finance Legislation Responding to Court Order." *Topeka Capital-Journal,* April 7.

Shorman, Jonathan. 2017. "Brownback Has National Ambitions for Kansas Welfare Policies." *Topeka Capital-Journal*, January 4.

Shorman, Jonathan. 2017a. "School Finance Formula to Provide Lawmakers with Daunting Task." *Topeka Capital-Journal*, January 3.

Shorman, Jonathan. 2017b. "Kansas Lawmakers Kick Off Tax Work by Offering Bill to Repeal LLC Exemption—Early Divide Seen over Making Tax Retroactive." *Topeka Capital-Journal,* January 9.

Shorman, Jonathan. 2017c. "Accountant Warns Kansas Lawmakers Partial Repeal of Business Tax Breaks Would Cause Confusion—Brownback Signals Openness to Compromise, Wants to Preserve 'Heart' of LLC Policy." *Topeka Capital-Journal,* January 17.

Shorman, Jonathan. 2017d. "KanCare Extension Denied after Scathing Review Finds Noncompliance with Federal Law—Kansas Hasn't Decided How to Respond to Denial but Is Preparing Corrective Action Plan." *Topeka Capital-Journal,* January 18.

Shorman, Jonathan. 2017e. "Kansas Supreme Court Rules School Funding Inadequate." *Topeka Capital-Journal*, March 2.

Spross, Jeff. 2017. "The GOP Plot to Drown Medicaid in the Bathtub." *The Week,* March 9. https://theweek.com/articles/684754/gop-plot-drown-medicaid-bathtub.

Wagoner, Jessie. 2014. "Republicans Take the State." *Emporia Gazette*, November 5.

Williamson, Kevin D. 2016. "Starving the Beast in Kansas." *National Review*, May 3. https://www.nationalreview.com/2016/05/kansas-tax-cuts-wont-starve-government-beast.

Woodall, Hunter. 2017. "Kansas Revenue Tops Estimates, but $342 Million Shortfall Still Looms." *Kansas City Star,* January 3.

Woodall, Hunter. 2017a. "Kansas Gov. Sam Brownback Offers Optimistic Vision in State of the State Address." *Kansas City Star*, January 10.

Woodall, Hunter. 2017b. "Kansas Supreme Court Rules New School Finance Formula Is Unconstitutional." *Kansas City Star.*

Chapter 8

Impact of the "Great Experiment"

Summary and Analysis

CHAPTER OVERVIEW

An overview of the shift in Kansas government provides an introduction to the Brownback years. The tax plan implemented during the 2012–2013 legislative sessions is reviewed, and results of that legislation are summarized. Using state and federal government data and analyses by economists, the authors assess the impact of Brownback's programs on the state and the reaction of segments of the population. Public education, human services, the economy and government services in general are examined; assessments by state leaders, economists, and political science experts are included.

HOW KANSAS GOVERNMENT CHANGED PRIOR TO THE BROWNBACK YEARS

The 2014 election apparently was an approval of the Brownback theory of government, which was described by John Marshall (2013), a journalist who wrote about Kansas politics for 40 years:

> Thus his [Brownback's] plan for a state with no income taxes; a state that rejects (some) federal aid; a state with legislation that squashes federal gun laws, dismantles revenue sharing for cities and counties, abolishes the Kansas Turnpike Authority, revokes paycheck dues collection by teacher unions, gives the governor sole authority to appoint appellate judges, and strikes most prohibitions from the state's open meetings law.

That election returned to Kansas a governor and legislature dominated by ultra-conservative lawmakers who believed that big government is the problem. That attitude, which followed the point of view often expressed by Ronald Reagan, was a departure from the perspective of previous generations of legislators in Kansas. As Marshall (ibid.) explained it, "For many generations, Kansans were governed by experienced, educated and thoughtful people who realized the great difference that government had made in their lives."

Prior to the twenty-first century, the three houses of Kansas government were made up primarily of men and women who had grown up on farms and in rural communities. Only a few came from bigger cities. Most knew what life was like before paved roads, electricity in the house, the telephone, and running water.

Legislators in earlier years believed that through government they could improve the lives of Kansans. As Marshall described it,

> With each generation, the roads were better, the water cleaner, the electricity reliable. There were wide highways and new schools, state parks and lakes, and conservation programs and crop insurance. There were new hospitals, flood control and programs to help with the mortgage. There were jobs, a minimum wage, and guaranteed insurance for bank accounts. There were school lunches. There were holidays.

The seeds of change in Kansas government can be traced to the policies of President Ronald Reagan. Reagan had proposed large cuts in federal government spending, and these reductions included cuts in federal aid for college students, programs for free or reduced-cost school lunches, some farm subsidies, welfare programs, Social Security, public health, defense, and even federal revenue sharing. This resolve to cut government spending found its way to Kansas two decades later.

However, as late as the 1990s, Kansas government continued to offer programs to benefit its citizens; the legislature established a new model for education funding; reformed social welfare programs to benefit poor families, children and the homeless; funded medical assistance for the poor; assisted the development of community mental health centers; increased aid to higher education; and passed a $14 billion highway improvement program.

That was during the 1990s. That all changed by 2013, and Marshall attributed the change partly to the composition of the Legislature: "It is a legislature largely inexperienced, heavily motivated, under-tested—all sketch and no blueprint."

Marshall claimed that some legislators who took office in the 2000s had not been tested in life. These younger legislators that dominated the legislature were from the cities and suburbs, products of a world of material wealth. They came from communities that already had good roads; they already had clean air and water. Their schools were new, and there were cell phones for all. Health care and poverty were not a problem where they lived.

A tide of conservatism carried Sam Brownback into office in 2010, further deepening the conservative majority in both House and Senate. Then, in the 2012 election, Brownback's conservative supporters were able to oust enough moderate Republicans to seize control of both houses of the Kansas Legislature.

Marshall noted that the prevailing philosophy of these conservatives was that people are responsible before God for their own lives, and government has little, if any, role to play in improving their lives. Under this new leadership, the legislature continued its efforts to minimize the role of government and to sever its relationship with the federal government. An example was Brownback's decision to refuse $31.5 million in federal assistance to establish a state health care exchange under the Affordable Care Act.

The Brownback plan was for a state with no income taxes, that dismantled revenue sharing for cities and counties, abolished the Kansas Turnpike Authority, outlawed the deduction of union dues from teachers' paychecks, granted the governor authority to appoint appellate judges (with a proposed constitutional amendment to also appoint Supreme Court judges), and cut funding for education at all levels. The state's Medicaid program, renamed "KanCare," was transferred to private companies.

The emphasis shifted from promoting services that improved life for Kansans to laws that supported a "business-friendly" environment. The underlying belief was that when businesses are making money, everybody benefits—the supply-side economic theory that is the basis for Brownback's "great experiment."

That is an overview of the transition that occurred during the first years of the Brownback administration. Now let's examine the impact of the Brownback agenda on the economy and services provided by Kansas government.

THE BROWNBACK ECONOMIC AGENDA

In 2012 Governor Brownback initiated the economic plan described in more detail in chapter 5. Here we summarize the major points in the governor's own words:

> Our new pro-growth tax policy will be like a shot of adrenaline into the heart of the Kansas economy. It will pave the way to the creation of tens of thousands of new jobs, bring tens of thousands of people to Kansas, and help make our state the best place in America to start and grow a small business. It will leave more than a billion dollars in the hands of Kansans. An expanding economy and growing population will directly benefit our schools and local governments.

> We will continue to work to provide a business environment that will keep our state regionally and globally competitive. We will continue to reform state government so that it is more efficient, effective and responsive to our citizens' needs. We will continue to meet the needs of our state's most vulnerable. We will continue to provide for high-quality schools. (Brownback 2012)

That economic agenda was employed during the second half of Brownback's first term as governor and continued unabated into the second term, which began in 2015. By 2017, the economic and social impact was apparent to Kansas citizens and to Kansas legislators. Here we describe the results of the plan supported by Governor Brownback and his colleagues in Kansas government.

ECONOMIC IMPACT OF THE BROWNBACK AGENDA

The impact of the 2012 tax cuts was evident the next fiscal year, as shown in table 8.1 and figure 8.1. Income tax receipts declined substantially in FY 2014, the first fiscal year that the Brownback tax cuts were in effect. In FY 2013 tax revenue was approximately $2.9 billion but dropped to $2.2 billion in FY 2014 and remained at the $2.2 to $2.3 billion level through the FY 2017.

A report from several public forums early in the 2017 legislature's term revealed both the social impact of the tax cuts and the response of some voters. Shorman (2017a) reported that attendees of a Pittsburg (KS) forum were unhappy that their senator did not attend. At other forums many citizens attended to thank their representatives who voted to support tax increases and to express disfavor for those who did not. Some attendees expressed concern for funding of higher education, which had been decreased. Others were concerned that legislation had been passed to allow concealed weapons on college campuses. School funding, Medicaid expansion and a failed effort to roll back the 2012 tax policy were often topics of the forums—the governor had vetoed a bill that would rollback the 2012 tax policy, and an override attempt passed

Table 8.1 State General Fund (Dollars in Billions)

	Income Tax Revenue	*Total Tax Revenue*
FY 2013	2.931	6.333
FY 2014	2.218	5.632
FY 2015	2.278	5.717
FY 2016	2.248	5.758
FY 2017	2.304	5.817
FY 2018 Estimate	2.927	6.385

Source: Duane Goossen. 2017. "Revenue Reset." *The Kansas Budget* (blog), September 12. http://www.kansasbudget.com/.

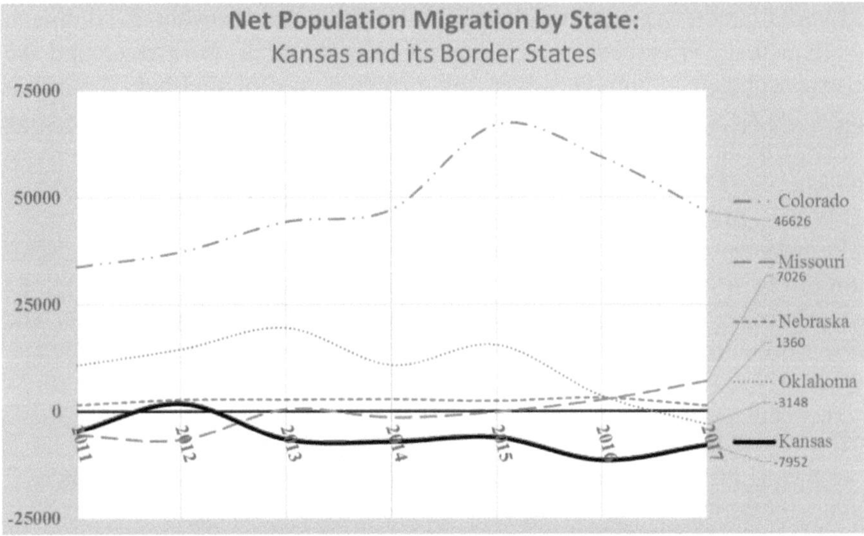

Figure 8.1 Net Population by State: Kansas and It's Border State (in figure). *Source*: Author.

the House of Representatives but fell three votes short of passing the Senate. One constituent was quoted as saying, "It seems we've had a really good experiment the last few years showing their philosophy doesn't work (ibid.)."

Other Kansans expressed concern that the Legislature had raided more than $1 billion from the state highway fund and had curtailed some highway projects. Some worried about the long-term impact on cuts in education and other areas of the budget. Still other citizens were upset with the state's credit rating—the state's credit rating had been downgraded several times. The result is higher interest rates for future bond issues.

The Kansas debt per capita in Kansas in 2016 was $1,534, while Moody's Investor Services reported that Missouri stood at $574, Colorado at $424, Oklahoma at $397 and Nebraska at $8 (ibid.).

Concern for higher education also appeared at numerous forums. In 2016 Brownback had cut state funds to public universities by 4 percent. As a result of cuts, adjunct faculty were being dumped, professors were experiencing more or larger classes, and universities were experiencing difficulty hiring faculty. University faculty had not received raises for several years, and some researchers were being enticed to other universities with the promise of higher salaries and the potential for merit raises.

The tax bill passed during the 2017 legislative session eliminated the LLC loophole, stopped the March to Zero (a formula in state law for future tax cuts), and moved income tax rates higher, though still below the rates in place before 2012.

Even after the legislature rolled back the tax cuts, Brownback continued to claim that his tax cuts were creating jobs for small businesses and the private sector generally. However, job growth lagged behind both the nation and neighboring states, and the decreased tax revenue forced Kansas to delay highway projects, cut allocations to higher education and other state services, and keep K-12 funding levels flat. Brownback blamed a decline in oil and agriculture prices for hurting revenue in the state.

Legislators in Kansas did not believe the governor's claims. At the conclusion of the 2017 legislative session, moderate Republican lawmakers joined with Democrats to override a Brownback veto and repeal the tax cuts. The New York Times chronicled the revolt by Brownback's fellow Republicans:

> The move amounted to a shocking rejection of the tax-cutting experiment Mr. Brownback had held up as the centerpiece of his conservative governing. But economic growth and revenues lagged, and even his allies began to publicly criticize the tax cuts. (Bowman et al. 2017)

Further, the *Times* characterized the rejection as "a warning of the risks for other Republican-controlled states" and "a dizzying descent for Mr. Brownback's legacy and any future political aspirations."

In an op-ed column in the *Topeka Capital-Journal*, Republican House Majority Leader Don Hineman provided a rationale for the veto override and a stark assessment of the Brownback program:

> The fiscal strain created by the 2012 tax cuts caused public schools to suffer, increasing class sizes and reducing program offerings. Medicaid reimbursements were reduced, straining rural hospital budgets heavily reliant on those payments. Highway funds for preservation and maintenance were cut to unsustainably low levels. And despite the assurances of adviser Art Laffer that economic nirvana was just around the corner, Kansans continued to move out of state. (Hineman 2017)

As majority leader and member of the House of Representatives for five terms, Mr. Hineman was a first-hand observer of the financial structure of Kansas before, during and after the Brownback economic plan. His support of the governor's veto as majority leader underscores the depth of concern for the elected officials in Kansas.

Duane Goossen (2017), former Kansas budget director under three governors, assessed the fiscal situation after four years of the Brownback fiscal plan:

> Gov. Brownback's tax experiment brought havoc to the Kansas budget, and put the state's general fund in severe financial distress. But in June, a bipartisan supermajority of lawmakers rescinded those policies in a dramatic veto override and put Kansas back on a more stable financial path.

In November 2017 the Kansas Legislative Research Department released a revised estimate of income for fiscal year 2017. Income tax receipts had dropped in FY 2014 because of the tax cuts implemented in 2012, but the repeal of these taxes resulted in a revised forecast of income tax revenue to $2.9 billion in FY 2018 (see table 8.1). Beginning in January 2017, "pass-through income" was once again subject to taxation. Also, sales tax receipts grew 4.4 percent over that same period the year before, and corporate income tax receipts grew almost 40 percent, accounting for the $568 million increase in tax revenue (from $5.817 million to $6.385 million) from FY 2017 to FY 2018. This increase was nearly 10 percent.

Five years into the Brownback tax plan, a study showed that, instead of "a shot of adrenalin," the tax plan had been a shot in the foot of the Kansas economy. An economic index produced by Emporia State University showed that Kansas' gross domestic product trailed that of most Midwest states the preceding year (Carpenter 2018). Economic activity growth during the period November 2016 to November 2017 was 1.03 percent in Kansas, trailing Oklahoma, Arkansas, Missouri, Nebraska, and Colorado, which registered increases ranging from 1.19 percent in Nebraska to 12.2 percent in Oklahoma. Iowa's increase was .9 percent. This monthly index bases GDP measurements on employment data, housing sales, oil prices, sales taxes, imports and exports, and a Philadelphia Federal Reserve assessment of economic activity.

According to this index, Kansas's GDP plateau began in 2014, one year after the Brownback tax cuts reduced income tax revenue. The $700 million drop in annual revenue resulted in budget deficits that resulted in a 2015 increase in the state sales tax and repeal of the earlier Brownback tax plan passed in 2012.

IMPACT ON STATE SERVICES

The Brownback administration frequently framed the tax cuts and small government in terms of savings to taxpayers with the promise that lower taxes would result in more revenue for businesses, which would invest in labor and benefit their workers. Smaller government, a required result of less tax revenue, was often couched in terms of "efficiencies." However, the results of less tax money could be documented by a review of government services following the implementation of the tax cuts of 2012 and 2013.

State Work Force Decreased

An analysis of workforce reports by *The Kansas City Star* revealed that the number of non-university state employees decreased nearly 25 percent between 2002 and 2016 (Ryan 2017). The reduction in the state workforce began during the terms of Democratic Governors Kathleen Sebelius and Mark Parkinson, which began with the Great Recession and concluded with the recession that followed 9/11. According to the *Star* report, the non-university state government workforce decreased 12 percent during those years.

During Brownback's six-year tenure, the number of state government workers decreased 14 percent. In 2016, the 17,000 non-university employees in state government were a loss of more than 5,600 workers since 2002. Furthermore, nearly every state agency reduced staff after 2002 because of a variety of factors, including reorganization, privatization (an emphasis during the Brownback years), cuts, and attrition.

The Kansas City Star analysis (ibid.) of data from the Kansas Department of Administration workforce personnel reports found that the agencies with the largest reductions were the following:

- Department of Children and Families (formerly called the Department of Social and Rehabilitation Services) down 1,800 staff members (49 percent);
- Department of Transportation down 1,050 workers (34 percent);
- Highway Patrol down 117 employees (14 percent);
- Adult correctional facilities reduced by 539 employees (20 percent); and
- State hospital staffs were reduced by 534 employees (25 percent).

This loss of staff also resulted in lost institutional knowledge, high turnover, and expertise. In comparison, the number of non-university government workers nationwide was stable during the period 2002–2006, and while the number of state workers nationwide declined following the recession, that decline was much less than that of Kansas. The reduction of state workers was part of the Brownback administration's philosophy of smaller government, although some staff reductions were unintended. According to Shawn Sullivan, state budget director, Larned State Hospital and Osawatomie State Hospital staffs have been reduced about 30 percent, but the problem primarily was difficulty recruiting workers in western Kansas.

A specific example of the impact on cutting staff and salaries arose from a report on nursing home inspections (*Topeka Capital-Journal* 2017a). Nursing facilities that receive Medicaid and Medicare funding are required to report to the state how they will correct deficiencies identified by inspections, and the state is responsible for ensuring that the required actions have been taken to address the problems. A federal review reported that the Kansas Department for Aging and Disability Services (KDADS) had failed to provide nursing homes' evidence of deficiencies identified in 2014 surveys. The U.S. Inspector General's Department of Health and Human Services Office found that the KDADS provided verification of correction of 48 deficiencies from a sample of 100 at 79 nursing homes. This report indicated that KDADS had established a practice of accepting nursing homes' correction plans as confirmation of compliance—without obtaining the required evidence of compliance.

KDADS representatives reported that one of the problems was lack of inspectors because at that time 13 of 61 KDADS positions were vacant, and the agency was working to increase inspectors' salaries. This situation, identified during the sixth year of the Brownback administration, is one example of a sometimes result of the "small government" philosophy applied to government administration. Services to the public can be damaged. In this case, senior citizens in nursing homes were denied adequate services.

The above examples are indicators of results when government is allowed or planned to shrink. An editorial in the *Topeka Capital Journal* (2017b) summarized issues that can accompany the move to smaller government and "efficiencies":

> Among many conservatives, there's a reflexive assumption that reducing the size of government is always a good thing. This is why politicians like Gov. Sam Brownback often declare their fervent opposition to "big government" and boast about their attempts to reduce spending, cull the number of state employees, etc. For example, Kansas budget director Shawn Sullivan says the Brownback administration made "an intentional effort to downsize, to be more efficient."

The impact was also felt by the Kansas Department of Corrections, which had lost 20 percent of its employees between 2002 and 2017. Furthermore, officers were paid less than the national average, and, as a result, there were 116 vacant position at Lansing and 93 at El Dorado (two correctional facilities) by the summer of 2017 (ibid.). Furthermore, the staff shortage required officers to work 12-hour or 16-hour shifts and El Dorado's turnover rate was reported at 46 percent. A result was inmate unrest—staff recorded 207 disciplinary incidents per month in 2016 and 362 during the first half of 2017.

The editorial concluded:

> Next time a politician mindlessly celebrates the diminution of government, just remember that state workers are the ones responsible for maintaining our roads, guarding our communities, securing our prisons and protecting our most vulnerable children.

State Pension System

Another detriment was the impact on the state's pension system. The pension fund for more than 100,000 state employees, the Kansas Public Employees Retirement System (KPERS), in 2015 had an unfunded actuarial liability of

$9 billion—the gap between the pension fund's resources and the amount need to pay benefits owed. In other words, the pension fund was 67 percent funded. In 2015 the state issued a $1 billion bond to pay expenses of the retirement fund. In 2016 the legislature delayed $100 million payment to the retirement system to be repaid in 2018 at 8 percent interest. The system has not increased its benefit amount to retirees for more than 20 years, and the legislature following the tax cuts yearly considered withholding from or deferring payments. By issuing a bond and by deferring payments, the governor and legislature while jeopardizing the long-term health of the pension fund were using the pension fund as a source for loans.

Child Welfare Services

Part of the Brownback effort to make government more efficient was to reorganize the Social and Rehabilitative Services (SRS) and to spin off the Department for Children and Families (DCF) to focus on child and family welfare issues. The governor's office delivered an executive order to the Kansas Legislature February 6, 2012. It was approved by the Legislature and implemented July 1, 2012. DCF is responsible for adult and child protective services, adoption, foster care, child support services, food assistance programs, vocational rehabilitation, and other services.

A report released by DCF in August 2018 revealed that the agency did not meet 16 of 30 federal and state performance standards during the period July 1, 2017, through June 30, 2018 (Associated Press 2018). Among data in the report was that children had 8.9 homes for every 1,000 days they were in foster care; the standard is for 4.12 homes every 1,000 days. Another standard missed: the agency assessed family needs within 30 days only 55 percent of the time, while the standard is 95 percent. The report found that children were adopted in less than two years 17.6 percent of the time, while the standard is nearly 27 percent.

Other standards missed: (1) children were kept in the same school 15.7 percent of the time when the standard requires at least 25 percent of the time and placing children in permanent homes within a year.

K–12 Education

Kansas schools also suffered from the tax cuts. A study by the nonpartisan Center on Budget and Policy Priorities reported that Kansas was among the six states with the greatest drop in per-pupil funding during the period 2008–2016, and five of those states had cut income taxes—Arizona, Idaho, Oklahoma, Wisconsin and Kansas (Albares 2016b). An analysis of the budgets showed that Kansas funding per student had fallen by 13 percent between 2008 and 2016, adjusting for inflation (ibid.). According to this source, such cuts result in increased class sizes, hiring less-qualified teachers, shortened school year, and fewer resources for students—all of which impede the fostering of a well-educated workforce.

In summation, the same policy analyst wrote, "Kansas' Supreme Court's ruling that the state isn't meeting its constitutional obligation to equitably fund its schools is the latest evidence of why Kansas is the poster child for the harm of large state tax cuts" (Albares 2016a). The reference is to a decision by the Kansas Supreme Court issued October 2, 2017. The Court instructed the Kansas Legislature to increase funding for public school districts and to prove its plan complies with the state constitution. The Supreme Court that school funding at that time was unconstitutional and ordered the Kansas Legislature to solve continuing problems with allocation of state aid to public education. The Court took issue with the amount the Legislature had appropriated and said that it did not measure up to the constitutional requirement of "adequacy" and "equity." The Court gave the legislature until April 30 of 2018 to submit briefs to remedy the funding formula.

Health Care

In 2013 Brownback implemented his privatized healthcare system in the state—KanCare, which serves more than 400,000 Kansans. The state run Medicaid system was replaced with a system of private health care companies. The change was beset with problems from the beginning—long waits for care and for health care providers to receive reimbursements. In 2016 the magnitude of the problems were publicized with a report from CMS (Shorman 2017b). In early 2017 the federal Centers for Medicare and Medicaid Services issued a report on concerns discovered during an on-site review of the program conducted in October 2016. The report claimed that Limited coordination between state agencies posed a risk to the health and safety of some participants in the program; furthermore, the state did not provide sufficient oversight of the privately run managed care organizations than ran the KanCare system. The KanCare system was found to be "substantively out of compliance" with U.S. law and posed risks to recipients. As a result, the state was denied extension of KanCare for a year. The report also indicated that the federal agency had received numerous complaints from beneficiaries, providers, and advocates. CMS required the state to implement an action plan to correct the identified deficiencies. Among the problems identified was a backlog exceeding 10,000 applications for service.

Highways

Kansas ranks fourth in the United States in terms of miles of public roads; Texas, California, and Illinois have more (U.S. Department of Transportation 2016). Highway construction and repair in Kansas suffered from the tax cuts.

In January 2017, Kansas Contractors Association Executive Vice President Bob Totten noted that during the period 2011–2016, $2.7 billion had been swept from the Kansas Department of Transportation. Totten warned, "By making the decision to virtually halt all new road and bridge projects, the administration has shown that it is willing to put up roadblocks on Kansas' future in order to patch budget holes it created" (Hawver 2017).

In that same article, Kansas Secretary of Transportation Richard Carlson said that his department would bid only $43 million in 2017 to provide about 235 miles of road maintenance jobs in the next fiscal year, down from more than $600 million in preceding years. In other words, the state was spending approximately seven percent on road maintenance compared to previous years—a recipe for infrastructure decay.

Migration

Among predictions immediately after passage of the 2012 tax plan was the assurance that a result would be reversal of the out-migration trend that had existed for decades. Nick Jordan, the state's revenue secretary, forecasted the creation of 22,000 more jobs and 35,000 more people moving into the state over the next five years (Cooper 2012).

According to Kansas Department of Labor statistics, the Kansas population grew from 2,858,850 in 2010 to 2,907,289 in 2016, an increase of 48,439 or 1.7 per cent. The U.S. population increased from 309,348,193 in 2010 to 323,127,513 in 2016, an increase of 4.45 percent.

Furthermore, census data showed that 9,000 more people left Kansas than moved to the state (Madden 2017). In a comparison with neighboring states, only Oklahoma lost more residents than Kansas (see table 8.2). Population losses for Arkansas and Nebraska were small, and two states gained populations—adjacent Missouri (7,062) and Iowa (78). Kansas and Oklahoma were outliers in population change during this period (see figure 8.1). After three years, the Brownback administration's forecast that 35,000 people would

Table 8.2 Population Change in Kansas and Adjoining States 2012–2017

State	*Population Change*
Arkansas	−135
Colorado	−4,352
Iowa	+78
Kansas	−9,099
Missouri	+7,062
Nebraska	−436
Oklahoma	−9,904

Source: Madden, Nathan. 2017. *Despite Promises, More Kansans Left the State after 2012 Income Tax Plan.* Kansas Center for Economic Growth, April 20.

move to Kansas in the five years following adoption of the tax plan was 44,000 short of the prediction.

Jobs

When campaigning in 2014 for his second term as governor, Brownback promised to create 100,000 private sector jobs. "Gov. Sam Brownback campaigned for re-election in 2014 by pledging to create 100,000 private-sector jobs during a second term in office." (Carpenter 2017).

The Kansas Department of Labor reported that the Kansas labor force decreased by 22,527 people in 2016, a decrease of 24,617 in employment and an increase of 2,090 in unemployment (Chilson 2017). Within that total, the state lost 9,300 nonfarm seasonally adjusted jobs in 2016.

Helling (2017) noted that Missouri created jobs nearly twice the rate of Kansas jobs since 2012. Furthermore, the nation's growth rate is nearly double the Kansas rate during the same time frame. There is ample evidence that the Brownback tax cuts were bad policy, but were they good politics?

BOND RATINGS LOWERED

Less than two years after the tax cuts were implemented, bond rating agencies noted the economic trends in Kansas and responded by downgrading the state's bond rating. In May 2014 Moody's Investor Services downgraded bond ratings citing the 2012 tax cuts. Then in August 2014 Standard and Poor's (S & P) lowered Kansas' bond rating from AA+ to AA and cited the state's unbalanced budget caused by the state's income tax cuts in 2012. An S & P credit analyst explained, "The downgrades reflect our view of a structurally unbalanced budget, following state income tax cuts that have not been matched with offsetting ongoing expenditure cuts in the fiscal 2015 budget" (Lowry 2014). The result is that the increased interest rates on bonds were issued at a time when balancing the budget was a major issue for state government.

The news of the S & P bond rating downgrade came shortly after the 2014 state primary election, and Governor Brownback was forced to confront this negative reflection on his tax plan. He accused the ratings agencies of making faulty analyses. "You know breaking addictions to high taxes is hard. That's a difficult thing to do. And that's what we're trying to do, is break addictions to high taxes," Brownback said "We will repay the bonds to investors. These are still high-grade bonds. . . . It is hard cutting taxes and we are doing it to create jobs. (ibid.)."

NATIONAL RANKING OF KANSAS IN 2018

In recent years *U.S. News and World Report* (2018) has ranked states on several measures, including health care, education, economy, opportunity, infrastructure, crime and corrections, fiscal stability, and quality of life. Each category is ranked based on surveys of people's rating of the most important factors in judging a state.

Table 8.3 displays a comparison of these factors for Kansas and adjoining states. Kansas ranks 29th among all states in these categories and among those states that adjoin Kansas, only Missouri and Oklahoma rank lower.

Kansas' best score in the state rankings, opportunity, ranked 12th in the nation. This category includes equality and affordability. The worst ranking was for the overall economy, which ranked 42nd among the 50 states. That category includes business environment, employment statistics and growth—all variables that the Brownback tax cuts were intended to bolster. The study found Kansas quality of life and infrastructure rated quite good, ranking the state 16th nationwide in both categories.

Kansas ranked 30th on health care, 37th in crime and corrections, and 37th, and 39th in fiscal stability. In the overall ranking, Kansas' 29th bested neighboring Missouri, ranked 30th, and Oklahoma, 43rd. The other two states adjoining Kansas, Nebraska and Colorado, both ranked in the top ten. Nebraska ranked seventh and Colorado tenth. It should be noted that Colorado had the highest ranking in the nation for its economy.

Kansas, however, ranked 42nd in the economy category. In the U.S. News and World Report rankings, economies were ranked by a number of measures that included employment, business environment and growth. Job growth and growth of each state's gross domestic product were measured between 2013 and 2016. Unemployment rate and participation in the labor force for everyone 16 and older also were measured. In addition, the number of people moving in and out of a state was taken into account. Business environment was considered, measured by overall tax burden, the number of top company headquarters per capita, venture capital disbursed, entrepreneurship and patent creation.

This national statistical ranking of states provides comparative information that appears to document the economic status of Kansas five years after implementation of the Brownback plan for the state. The rankings for economy (42nd) and fiscal stability (39th) and overall ranking (29th) nationally suggest economic problems.

Regionally, Kansas shares a border with Colorado, Oklahoma, Nebraska, and Missouri. Figure 8.2 illustrates the relative changes of these neighboring states by using converting each state's GDP into an index number of 100 for 2011, which is the year Sam Brownback was inaugurated as the Governor of

Table 8.3 2018 *U. S. News* Rankings of Kansas and Adjoining States

Category	*Kansas*	*Nebraska*	*Colorado*	*Missouri*	*Oklahoma*
Health care	30	19	9	39	48
Education	21	9	20	25	39
Economy	42	21	1	33	36
Opportunity	12	13	28	21	38
Infrastructure	16	9	14	20	31
Crime & corrections	37	19	29	45	34
Fiscal stability	39	11	31	10	22
Quality of life	16	14	10	15	17
Overall ranking	29	7	10	30	43

Source: U.S. News and World Report. 2018. *Best States Rankings*. https://www.usnews.com/news/best-states/rankings.

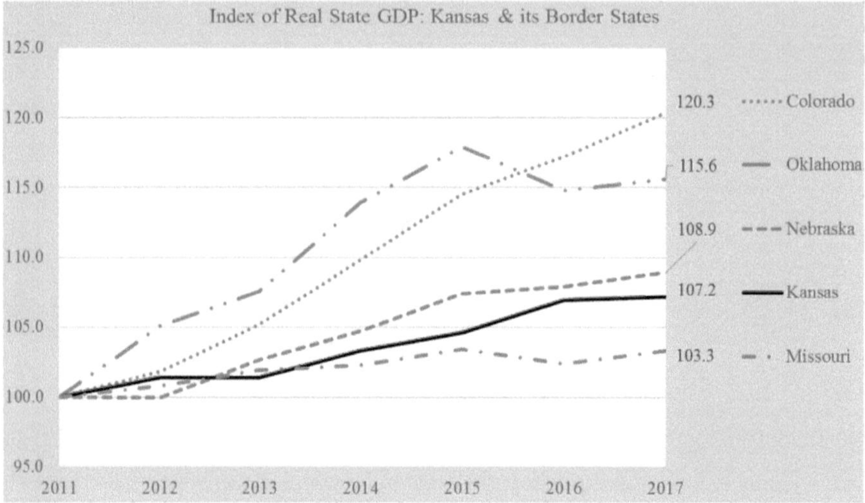

Figure 8.2 Index of Real Estate GDP: Kansas & its Border state (in figure). *Source*: Author.

Kansas. The graph further illustrates that the Kansas economy lagged behind neighboring states during the Brownback years.

IMPACT ON BROWNBACK'S POPULARITY

While the economy flagged during Brownback's tenure as governor, his popularity also declined. A February 2010 Rasmussen poll, before Brownback's campaign for governor, indicated Sam Brownback's favorable rating was 58 percent, and only 34 percent saw him unfavorably.

Six years later, in the fall of 2016, Brownback's favorable rating had declined to 23 percent—a decrease of 35 points. The most probable explanation is Kansans' displeasure with the tax cuts (Helling 2017). Perhaps the reason is that Kansans were not asking for a tax cut, and they blamed him for the spending cuts to education, road maintenance, and other state programs.

In the final analysis, the Brownback plan for Kansas was both bad economic policy and bad politics. The economy of the state suffered, as indicated above, and the governor's popularity suffered as well.

BROWNBACK LEAVES KANSAS BEHIND

In July 2017, two months after the Kansas Legislature overrode the governor's veto of his tax plan's repeal, President Donald Trump nominated

Brownback to serve as the next ambassador at large for international religious freedom, but the confirmation stalled in the Senate. The Senate Foreign Relations Committee narrowly advanced Brownback's nomination in October by a party-line vote of 11–10 after concerns were raised about his record on gay rights. Brownback responded to questions posed by Democrats during the committee hearing that he would continue U.S. efforts to protect the rights of persecuted groups and minorities, including lesbian, gay and transgendered individuals.

Anticipating the appointment, Brownback began the process of transferring government duties to his lieutenant governor, Jeff Colyer, who appointed a new secretary for the Department for Children and Families and took an active role developing the governor's annual budget. However, Brownback delivered the budget and the annual State of the State address January 9, 2018.

In that address, Brownback called for an additional $600 million in school funding over five years as the Kansas Legislature was trying to pass a school finance formula that the Kansas Supreme Court would accept as constitutional. However, Brownback's budget did not indicate how would pay for $600 million proposed increase. Even Republican leaders recoiled at the proposal as well as other lofty goals in his State of the State address: a 95 percent statewide graduation rate, at least 75 percent of Kansas students should be continuing their education after graduation, accelerate the movement of Kansas schools to the Kansans Can model for school redesign launched by the Kansas Department of Education and five objectives to meet those goals within five years: (1) a higher average teacher pay than any of our surrounding states, (2) increase the number of school counselors and school psychologists in Kansas schools by 150 positions each year, (3) have at least 50 schools participating in the Kansans Can school redesign project, (4) every Kansas high school should offer at least 15 credit hours of dual credit coursework to every high school student, at no additional cost to parents, and (5) they should also offer every Kansas high school student, at no additional cost to parents, the choice of taking either the ACT college entrance exam or the Work Keys assessment.

Following the speech, *The Kansas City Star* noted the negative reaction by legislators and quoted Senate President Susan Wagle, a Wichita Republican: "I think he's lost a lot of trust from the Legislature and the electorate" (Woodall 2018).

On January 24 the U.S. Senate voted narrowly to confirm Brownback ambassador-at-large for international religious freedom, a post in the U.S. Department of State. The Senate vote had deadlocked at 49–49, and Vice President Mike Pence cast the tie-breaking vote.

A *Wichita Eagle* (2018) editorial described the general reaction of both legislators and the general public as Brownback left the state in limbo while he waited for his appointment in the Trump administration but clung to his power as governor, even giving a State of the State Address when it was clear to legislators and the public that he would leave as soon as confirmed:

> But Brownback couldn't let go, so his speech and budget proposal become a prime example for his years as governor. He tried to lead but failed. He offered fixes mired in fantasy. His legacy becomes galvanizing Kansans—many who voted twice for him—into knowing they can do better.

Perhaps that succinct statement best summarizes the legacy of Sam Brownback, who resigned a safe U.S. Senate seat to run for governor, apparently to bolster his run for the presidency. His "great experiment" failed, leaving the state on the brink of bankruptcy, and polling showed his popularity second lowest among all U.S. governors.

If California and Massachusetts are regarded as evidence that supply-side economic theory is the key to prosperity in the states, Sam Brownback's "great experiment" in Kansas provided economic and social data that shows how the supply-side economic theory can produce negative results. Many factors must be considered when shaping economic policy, and the advice of experts (plural) should be consulted to provide various points of view when a theory like supply-side economics is employed on a large scale. It is apparent that the Kansas experiment went awry when quick political decisions were made that greatly impacted the intent to stimulate the economy. Once again, it appeared that moderation would have been prudent, but prudence gave way to a desire to win a political victory.

CHAPTER SUMMARY

Sam Brownback led a radical reshaping of the Kansas tax structure, implementing supply-side economic principles that would cut taxes for the purpose of increasing productivity while imposing efficiencies in state government. Using state and federal government data and analyses by economists, the authors assessed the impact of Brownback's programs on the state and the reaction of segments of the population. Contrary to predicted outcomes, the tax cuts imposed in 2012 and 2013 substantially decreased state revenue, resulting in cuts to education, the state workforce, and state services. To balance the budget, money was borrowed from the state pension fund and taken from gasoline taxes generated for highway maintenance and construction. The revenue decrease resulted in lowering of bond ratings, and the promise of new businesses moving to the state along with population increase went unfulfilled. The "great experiment" did not produce the results predicted by

Brownback and his supporters; the disappointing results of the governor's plan resulted in Brownback's loss of popularity within his own party and among his constituents.

REFERENCES

Albares, Nick. 2016a. *Kansas: More Evidence of the Harm of Large Tax Cuts.* Center on Budget and Policy Priorities, February 12. https://www.cbpp.org/blog/kansas-more-evidence-of-the-harm-of-large-tax-cuts.

Albares, Nick. 2016b. *Steep Tax Cuts Endanger School Funding, in Kansas and Elsewhere.* Center on Budget and Policy Priorities, February 17. https://www.cbpp.org/blog/steep-tax-cuts-endanger-school-funding-in-kansas-and-elsewhere.

Associated Press. 2018. "Kansas Child Welfare Agency Failed to Meet 16 Standards." *The Emporia Gazette*, September 1 and 2, p. 8.

Bowman, Julie, Mitch Smith, and Monica Davey. 2017. "Brownback Tax Cuts Set Off a Revolt by Kansas Republicans." *The New York Times*, June 7.

Brownback, Sam. 2012. "Tax Cuts Needed to Grow the Economy." *The Wichita Eagle,* July 29.

Carpenter, Tim. 2017. "Kansas Loses 5,300 Private-Sector Jobs; Jobless Rate Holds at 3.7%." *Topeka Capital-Journal,* June 16.

Carpenter, Tim. 2018. "New GDP Index Shows Kansas Struggling to Keep Pace with Rival States." *The Topeka Capital-Journal,* January 28.

Chilson, Morgan. 2017. "Kansas Down 9,400 Private Sector Jobs in 2016." *The Topeka Capital-Journal,* January 20.

Cooper, Brad. 2012. "Brownback Signs Big Tax Cut in Kansas." *The Kansas City Star*, May 23. http://www.kansascity.com/latest-news/article303137/Brownback-signs-big-tax-cut-in-Kansas.html.

Goossen, Duane. 2017. *Revenue Reset.* Kansas Center for Economic Growth, September 6. https://realprosperityks.com/goossen-revenue-reset/.

Hawver, Martin. 2017. "Highway Projects Shrink Away." *Hawver's Capitol Report,* January 24.

Helling, Dave. 2017. "What Congress Can Learn From Sam Brownback: Kansas Tax Cuts Were Bad Policy and Bad Politics." *The Kansas City Star*, October 24.

Hineman, Don. 2017. "Why Tax Reform Was Necessary." *The Topeka Capital-Journal*, July 3.

Lowry, Brian. 2014. "S & P Downgrades Kansas Bond Rating; Brownback Pushes Back." *Wichita Eagle,* August 6.

Madden, Nathan. 2017. *Despite Promises, More Kansans Left the State after 2012 Income Tax Plan.* Kansas Center for Economic Growth, April 20. https://realprosperityks.com/despite-promises-kansans-left-state-2012-income-tax-plan/.

Mankiw, N. Gregory. 2017. "A '70s Economic Theory Comes to Life Once More." *The New York Times*, A19, April 25.

Marshall, John. 2013. "A New Confederacy." Kansas Health Institute. Archives: *KHI News Service*, May 18. http://www.khi.org/news/article/new-confederacy.

Ryan, Kelsey. 2017. "Under Brownback, Kansas Government Kept Shrinking. 'We've Got a Lot of Damage to Repair.'" *The Kansas City Star*, October 18.

Shorman, Jonathan. 2017a. "Kansans Urge Lawmakers to Push on Amid Fights over Taxes, Schools." *Topeka Capital-Journal,* March 5.

Shorman, Jonathan. 2017b. "KanCare Extension Denied after Scathing Review Finds Noncompliance with Federal Law." *Topeka Capital-Journal,* January 18.

Topeka Capital-Journal. 2017a. "Editorial: State Needs to Protect Seniors." September 14.

Topeka Capital-Journal. 2017b. "Editorial: State Employees Do Crucial Work." October 22.

U.S. Department of Transportation. 2016. *Highway Statistics: Highway Infrastructure, Public Road Mileage by Functional System* (Table HM-20). Federal Highway Administration. http://www.fhwa.dot.gov/policyinformation/statistics/2016.

U.S. News and World Report. 2018. *Best States Rankings.* https://www.usnews.com/news/best-states/rankings.

Wichita Eagle. 2018. "Brownback Leaves Details to Others." Editorial Board. January 11.

Woodall, Hunter. 2018. "Facing Republican Wrath, Gov. Brownback Fights for Relevance." *The Kansas City Star*, January 16.

Chapter 9

Assessment of the "Great Experiment"

CHAPTER OVERVIEW

Following Sam Brownback's unsuccessful bid for presidency in 2008, he left his position in the U.S. Senate to conduct a successful campaign in his home state of Kansas. Successful in that campaign, he apparently sought to build a case for his qualifications to be president of the United States. He outlined in his first State of the State Address in January 2011 that he would grow the Kansas economy; spend more money on education, which he described as "the state's primary function"; reform state government by delivering core services in "innovative and more efficient ways"; protect families by addressing healthcare needs; and "help those in their time of need" including protecting the unborn.

The decision that impacted this agenda was his plan to cut taxes in order to boost the economy and to "reform state government." Contrary to predicted outcomes, the tax cuts imposed in 2012 and 2013 substantially decreased state revenue, resulting in cuts to education, the state workforce, and state services—negating the goals that he had set.

In chapter 8 we outlined the results of the tax cuts: money was borrowed from the state pension fund and taken from gasoline taxes generated for highway maintenance and construction. The revenue decrease resulted, among other things, in lowering of bond ratings, and the promise of new businesses moving to the state along with population increase was unfulfilled. The "Great Experiment" did not produce the results predicted by Brownback and his supporters.

In this chapter we provide a summary of the "Great Experiment's" effects on state services and our analysis of the Brownback plan and its impact as we see it following Brownback's departure from the state.

RESULTS OF THE BROWNBACK PLAN

In chapter 8 the authors provided an analysis of the Brownback plan's impact on the economy, work force, and state programs. Below is a brief summary.

Economic Impact

Five years into the Brownback tax plan, a study showed that, instead of "a shot of adrenalin," the tax plan had a negative impact on the economy. An economic index produced by Emporia State University showed that Kansas' gross domestic product trailed that of most Midwest states the preceding year (Carpenter 2018).

State Work Force

During Brownback's six-year tenure, the number of state government workers decreased 14 percent. This loss of staff also resulted in lost institutional knowledge, high turnover, and expertise. Reducing size of government had definite effects on the quality of public services.

State Pension System

The Kansas Public Employees Retirement System (KPERS) is a pension fund for more than 100,000 state employees. The system has not increased its benefit amount to retirees for more than 20 years. After the 2012 tax cuts, the governor and legislature issued a bond and deferred payments to the pension system, jeopardizing the long-term health of the pension fund while using the pension fund as a source for loans.

K–12 Education

A study by the nonpartisan Center on Budget and Policy Priorities reported that Kansas was among the six states with the greatest drop in per-pupil funding during the period 2008–2016. An analysis of the budgets showed that Kansas funding per student had fallen by 13 percent between 2008 and 2016, adjusting for inflation (Albares 2016). According to this source, such cuts result in increased class sizes, hiring less-qualified teachers, shortened school year, and fewer resources for students—all of which impede the fostering of a well-educated workforce. The Kansas Supreme Court on October 2, 2017, instructed the Kansas Legislature to increase funding for public school districts and to prove its plan complies with the state constitution.

Child Welfare Program

Part of the Brownback effort to make government leaner was to create the Department for Children and Families (DCF), which had been part of Social and Rehabilitative Services (SRS). The DCF mission is to focus on child and family welfare issues. A report released by DCF in August 2018 revealed that the agency did not meet 16 of 30 federal and state performance standards during the period of July 1, 2017, through June 30, 2018 (Associated Press 2018). Missing more than half of the standards was a strong indicator that the department was not adequately fulfilling its mission.

Health Care

In 2013 Brownback implemented his privatized healthcare system in the state—KanCare, which serves more than 400,000 Kansans. The change was beset with problems from the beginning—long waits for care and for healthcare providers to receive reimbursements. In early 2017 the federal Centers for Medicare and Medicaid Services issued a report on concerns discovered during an on-site review of the program conducted in October 2016 (Shorman 2017). The KanCare system was found to be "substantively out of compliance" with U.S. law and posed risks to recipients. As a result, the state was denied extension of KanCare for a year. Among the problems identified was a backlog exceeding 10,000 applications for service.

Highways

Highway construction and repair also suffered from the tax cuts. During the period 2011–2016, $2.7 billion had been swept from the Kansas Department of Transportation. Kansas Secretary of Transportation Richard Carlson said that his department would bid only $43 million in 2017 to provide about 235 miles of road maintenance jobs in the next fiscal year, down from more than $600 million in preceding years (Hawver 2017). The result was placing the highway system at risk for the foreseeable future.

Migration

Among predictions immediately after passage of the 2012 tax plan was the assurance that a result would be reversal of the out-migration trend that had existed for decades; however, census data showed that 9,000 more people left Kansas than moved to the state during the period 2013–2015 (Madden 2017). In comparison with neighboring states, only Oklahoma lost more residents than Kansas (see table 8.2).

During the years Brownback was governor, Kansas generally had more migration out of the state compared with its neighbors (see figure 8.1).

Jobs

When campaigning in 2014 for his second term as governor, Brownback promised to create 100,000 private sector jobs. The Kansas Department of Labor reported that the Kansas labor force decreased by 22,527 people in 2016, a decrease of 24,617 in employment and an increase of 2,090 in unemployment (Chilson 2017). Within that total, the state lost 9,300 nonfarm seasonally adjusted jobs in 2016. Helling (2017) noted that Missouri created jobs nearly twice the rate of Kansas jobs since 2012. Furthermore, the nation's growth rate is nearly double the Kansas rate during the same time frame.

Figure 9.1 illustrates the relative growth of nonfarm employment of Kansas compared with the states that border it. The index of each state is set to 100 for January 2011. By November 2018, which was the latest data available due to the partial U.S. government shutdown in early 2019, data indicated that employment in Kansas was up 106.9 percent from January 2011 (i.e., employment grew by 6.9 percent over this time span in Kansas). The comparable November 2018 index numbers are illustrated next to each state in rank order from highest (Colorado) to lowest (Kansas). Growth in nonfarm employment in Kansas lagged behind all of its border states.

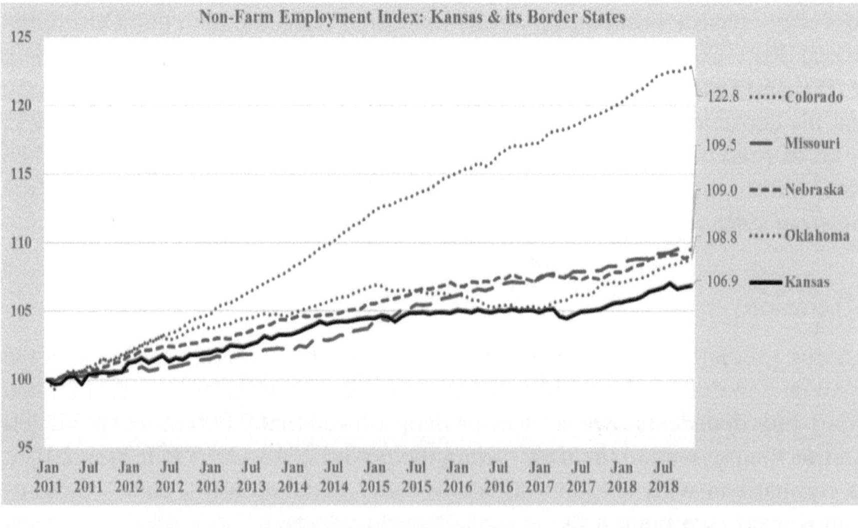

Figure 9.1 Nonfarm Employment Index: Kansas and its Border States. *Source*: Author.

Bond Ratings Lowered

Less than two years after the tax cuts were implemented, bond rating agencies noted the economic trends in Kansas and responded by downgrading the state's bond rating (Lowry 2014). In May 2014 Moody's Investor Services downgraded bond ratings citing the 2012 tax cuts. Then in August 2014 Standard and Poor's lowered Kansas' bond rating from AA+ to AA and cited the state's unbalanced budget caused by the state's income tax cuts in 2012.

National Ranking of Kansas in 2018

In recent years U.S. News and World Report has ranked states on several measures, including health care, education, economy, opportunity, infrastructure, crime and corrections, fiscal stability, and quality of life. Each category is ranked based on surveys of people's rating of the most important factors in judging a state.

This national statistical ranking of states provides comparative information that appears to document the economic status of Kansas five years after the implementation of the Brownback plan for the state. The rankings for economy (42nd) and fiscal stability (39th) and overall ranking (29th) nationally suggest economic problems (U.S. News and World Report 2018).

Ample evidence exists that the Brownback plan, based on Laffer's supply-side economic theories, did not work in Kansas. How can the plan's failure be explained? The authors provide their assessment below.

WHAT WENT WRONG

In our analysis of the Kansas "great experiment," we suggest the following issues were responsible for the plan's failure: (1) The "experiment" did not follow the Laffer theory; (2) the income from tax cuts at the state level was not adequate to boost the economy; (3) Brownback and his staff should have recognized the obvious problems in the legislation and Brownback should have refused to sign the outlandish tax package; (4) diverting money from the highway and pension funds was borrowing from the future; delaying needed road repairs, placing the road infrastructure in peril for the foreseeable future and endangering retirement benefits for state workers; (5) Brownback was unable to admit that his plan failed—even as he left the state. Each of these issues is addressed below.

1. The Laffer theory was not fully understood when implemented.

   Governor Brownback hired economist Arthur Laffer to provide guidance for his "great experiment" to cut taxes in order to boost the economy. The Laffer Curve suggests that tax rates can enhance economic activity or discourage it by lowering or raising taxes. Whether a tax cut will raise or lower revenues depends upon several variables: (1) the tax system already in place when the new tax rate is implemented, (2) the time period, (3) tax loopholes available, and (4) the ease with which businesses can move into "underground activities." When individuals and businesses are considering their "bottom line," they will make decisions that will put money into their pockets or the coffers of their business. Although a person may be willing to support government activity for the common good, most people will try to avoid paying more taxes than required by law.

As noted in chapter 7, tax rates are not exact predictors of revenue to be gained; raising a tax by 50 percent would not necessarily increase revenue by 50 percent because that increase will have an impact that might diminish incentives for work production and investment that would result in less revenue than the arithmetic would suggest. Similarly, the Laffer Curve suggests that lowering taxes could be an incentive for production and investment, and the result would be revenue more than predicted by an arithmetic computation. However, other factors must be considered. There is more to supply-side economic theory than lowering income taxes to create economic growth. Lowering income taxes works when other economic growth stimuli are at work. For example, the Kennedy tax cuts of 1961 were implemented when the highest marginal income tax rates were decreased from 91 percent to 70 percent. The 91 percent rate was imposed to help finance United States participation in World War II and to keep people from getting rich from the war effort, but the war had ended, and there was no need for the revenue generated by the high tax rate. Also, tens of thousands of GIs returned to civilian life, many with a college education subsidized by the federal government. The economy was strong and responsive to the stimulus of a tax cut.

During the Reagan administration, the tax cut led to robust and enduring economic growth, but taxes also were raised during the Reagan administration. In addition, Reagan was willing to increase the national debt during his administration, and the economic climate was right for the tax cuts to stimulate the economy as intended.

George W. Bush also cut taxes on income, capital gains, and dividends in 2003, but this move was made after entering the wars in Iraq and Afghanistan, which also helped to stimulate the economy. The tax cuts, combined with military spending on the two wars, promoted a flourishing economy—a boom that ended in 2008 with the most serious recession in the United States since the Great Depression.

There are also examples at the state level when supply-side principles were employed to stimulate a state's economy. In the late 1970s, California faced a massive growth spurt. Property taxes were very high and were reduced with the passage of Proposition 13. The reduced taxes encouraged workers to migrate to the state to take jobs that were being created, and the economy grew. California, with the juxtaposition of tax cuts and job growth, particularly in the electronics industry, became a success story for the Laffer theory. Similarly, Massachusetts, a hub of the financial world, at the time a growth industry, benefitted from reductions in both property and capital gains taxes.

The success stories noted above are evidence that one must consider the "big picture" of tax revenue. Although tax rates are a fundamental part of supply-side economic theory, other aspects are part of the bigger economy picture including free trade, stable prices, regulation that does not hinder industry, welfare policies that encourage work, and a reasonably open immigration policy.

The "big picture of the economy" includes a value system that supports business and a flourishing economy; however, the economy must be seen as an integral part of society that includes quality of life, social equality, minority rights, labor, and all contributing to "the common good." Corporate interests alone cannot be the overriding force that drives the policies and laws that provide the ethical and legal framework for the conduct of business. Ultimately, the overall quality of life in a democratic society must be the common goal.

In Kansas the government is funded primarily through three sources—income tax, property tax, and sales tax. The three sources must be balanced, and these revenue sources are often characterized as a "three-legged stool." The three legs of the stool must be approximately balanced, or the stool will not stand; it will be unbalanced and teeter perilously.

The Brownback tax package passed by the legislature in 2012 eliminated the income tax from LLCs—limited liability corporations. As a result approximately 330,000 business entities did not pay income tax, costing the state a considerable amount of revenue. That change in the tax rate resulted in income tax receipts to decline substantially in FY 2014, the first fiscal year that the tax cuts were in effect. In FY 2013 tax revenue was approximately $2.9 billion but dropped to $2.2 billion in FY 2014 and remained at the $2.2 to $2.3 billion level through the FY 2017. Consequently, the state budget lost approximately $701 million in 2014, $616 million in 2015, $575 million in 2016, and $516 million in 2017. This loss of approximately $2.41 billion in four years caused a budget crisis in the state. There was little evidence that the tax cuts were "a shot of adrenalin" to the economy.

Apparently, the governor and his staff, when developing the tax cut package, did not consider the complexity of the state's economics, nor did they consider the "big picture" of the goal to provide for the "common good" of the state. Instead, the governor and his supporting leadership team employed a simplistic approach based on the Laffer theory. The result was a decimated state budget that would take many years to recover.

2. Brownback should not have signed the tax package.

   Passage of the 2012 tax bill that implemented the elimination of income tax for some business owners and ignited the budget woes in Kansas was a political soap opera. A major role in that event was played by Steve Morris, president of the Kansas Senate. In an interview (Carpenter 2015), Morris recalled that in March 2012, he led an effort by moderate Republicans and Democrats in the Senate to join in defeating a tax reform bill on a 20-20 vote. Governor Brownback then phoned Morris, who left the Senate floor to take the call from the governor. Brownback asked Morris to orchestrate another vote on the bill.

   In response to the governor, Morris persuaded enough moderate Republicans to switch their votes and vote to support the tax-cut measure that was not to be the final version, Morris said. Morris understood that the governor intended to provide House and Senate negotiators a plan for a compromise that would not devastate the state budget.

   However, in May 2012, Brownback signed the Senate bill and denied offering assurances to Morris of waiting for an alternative plan.

   Brownback did not get the "pay-fors" that would have produced some of the revenue lost by the tax cuts, and it was apparent to most legislators that the plan would pay for itself only if the economy received a substantial boost from the tax cuts—and that boost was unlikely. Morris, by his admission, was bending to the will of the governor and his assurance that a better tax plan would be worked out, but the governor signed the bill. We have to ask: Why? What was Governor Brownback thinking?

3. Revenue lost from income taxes was not compensated with other revenue

   In 2013, the fiscal year that the tax cut was passed, $2.9 billion was collected in income taxes, and the total tax income was $13.48 billion—income tax accounted for 21.5 percent of revenue. In fiscal year 2014, income tax revenue was $2.2 billion and total income was $13.13 billion or 16.8 percent of revenue. Later, in fiscal year 2017, income tax revenue was $2.3 billion and the total revenue was 13.85 billion or 16.6 percent.

The loss of nearly one-fifth of income tax revenue in the first year of the tax cut was not compensated with other revenue, and that loss continued until the legislature overturned Brownback's veto in 2017 in order to reinstate the income taxes from LLCs. Had the leadership addressed the loss of revenue and identified alternative sources of revenue—even moderate tax increases on such items as fuel, vehicles, cigarettes and tobacco, liquor and beer, severance, or insurance premiums—the revenue loss could have been overcome. Instead, the loss of income tax revenue was supplanted by raiding money that was intended for such staples as road construction and repair and retirement benefits for state workers that would eventually need to be replenished.

4. Diverting money from the highway fund and retirement system was borrowing from the future.

   Gas tax revenue was a tempting target for administration and legislators seeking to stop the hemorrhaging of the state budget following the tax cuts. The removal of funds for road repairs in the state would not be noticed by taxpayers immediately, even though the amount invested in road construction and repair was cut drastically. It was only after several years had passed that the potholes and cracked pavement on heavily travelled roads were quite literally felt by drivers and passengers throughout the state. The billions of dollars directed away from road maintenance and construction would not be replaced for many years, and the state's highway infrastructure had been set back several years and impacted travel, shipping, and postal delivery.

   Similarly, money borrowed from the state retirement system would have to be repaid in order to pay the retirement benefits promised to state workers. In 2015 the state issued a $1 billion bond to pay expenses of the retirement fund, thereby putting off the payment and adding the interest required for a number years, increasing the amount paid by the state. In 2016 the legislature delayed $100 million payment to the retirement system to be repaid in 2018 at 8 percent interest—again adding to the cost of paying for retirement income. The governor and legislature jeopardized the long-term health of the pension fund for the short-term purpose of plugging financial gaps created by the tax cuts.

5. Brownback was unable to admit that his plan failed.

   During his second term as governor the effects of his economic agenda showed clearly that the tax cuts fell short of their intent to be a "shot of adrenalin" to the economy. But Brownback blamed first the Obama administration, then the poor farm economy for the economic downturn—ignoring the tax plan that he pushed. His 2018 State of the State Address, delivered weeks before he resigned his office, is evidence of his unwillingness to admit defeat.

Early in the address, Brownback listed the following as the highlights in Kansas during 2017:

- A record for most Kansans ever employed, 1.4 million, and the lowest unemployment rate since 2000;
- Opening of the longest hiking and biking trail in the state;
- In 2016, Kansas was the only state in the nation to reduce its rate of adult obesity;
- The state's childhood poverty rate is the lowest level since before the Great Recession;
- The infant mortality rate is the lowest point in history;
- A new state-of-the-art medical education building was opened at the University of Kansas Medical Center, expected to educate an additional 50 doctors each year;
- The biggest milk drying facility in the United States was opened in Garden City;
- The American Royal [a Kansas City MO nonprofit organization that sponsors livestock shows and other events to support scholarships for youth] is moving to Kansas;
- Saw the completion of the new National Soccer Training Center in Kansas City;
- "Our quail population is back, with the highest levels in 20 years";
- The state's "wind energy industry continues to grow dramatically with nearly 30 percent of our electricity now coming from the wind."

Not mentioned was the revolt in the Kansas Legislature—an override of his veto—that terminated the disastrous income tax exemptions given to 300,000 businesses. Of course, he did not mention his plummeting popularity, which made him the second most unpopular governor in the United States. Also not mentioned is the recognition that most of the highlights that he cited were not directly, or even indirectly, related to his or the state's programs.

The Brownback "experiment" applied a complex economic theory in a simplistic manner, was signed into law hastily with little consideration for long-term impact, lacking adequate income to defray the tax cuts that were the centerpiece of the plan, required the depletion of budgets for highways and the public retirement system, and Mr. Brownback refused to accept the errors, only prolonging resolution of the problems and lengthening the time required for the state's economic recovery. Much of the anxiety and suffering caused by this "experiment gone wrong" could have been avoided with careful, thoughtful leadership.

CONCLUSION

The low-tax/small-government philosophy has been a staple among conservatives and probably will continue to be. Sam Brownback's effort to employ these concepts in Kansas as a "real live experiment" in his apparent effort to show his qualifications to be President of the United States was a failed experiment.

As Sam Brownback was awaiting endorsement by the U.S. Senate to accept his appointment as Ambassador for Religious Freedom, the *Topeka Capital-Journal* recognized that Brownback, a native Kansan, had good intentions when he implemented his plan, but the results were far from favorable:

> So yes, absolutely, Sam Brownback had the interests of Kansans at his heart when he set forth goals for his administration. However, Brownback's signature plan to cut taxes, which he labeled a "real live experiment,'' exploded into something far too detrimental for the state. Basic services were cut, public schools lacked funding and revenue projections often fell short. Eventually, the Republican's tax policies were rejected by moderate members of his own party, who joined with Democrats to override the governor's veto last year on a measure to increase taxes in an attempt to restore state funds.
>
> While Brownback won reelection, his popularity has declined greatly in his second term as the lower tax burden he imposed on businesses never spurred the economic growth he envisioned with his tax measures. (Capital-Journal Editorial Board 2018)

We approached this Kansas experiment as a case study, and as pointed out in this chapter, numerous mistakes were made in the implementation. Arthur Laffer has collected data for many years in support of his "Laffer Curve" theory, and he has clearly stated the complexity that is associated with cutting taxes in order to stimulate a nation's or state's economy. Cutting taxes will indeed stimulate a nation's or a state's economy when the conditions are right and when accommodations are made for providing revenue that will support desired services provided by government.

The Kansas experiment does not disprove the Laffer theory or discredit the low-tax/small-government ideology. However, the Kansas experiment is a case study that suggests that cutting taxes must be done after careful study and with careful planning. The Kansas experiment is a case study in how NOT to cut taxes in order to stimulate the economy while making government more efficient. Kansas has provided a cautionary tale for political leaders.

REFERENCES

Albares, Nick. 2016. *Steep Tax Cuts Endanger School Funding, in Kansas and Elsewhere*. Center on Budget and Policy Priorities, February 17. https://www.cbpp.org/blog/steep-tax-cuts-endanger-school-funding-in-kansas-and-elsewhere.

Associated Press. 2018. "Kansas Child Welfare Agency Failed to Meet 16 Standards." *The Emporia Gazette*, September 1 and 2, p. 8.

Carpenter, Tim. 2015. "High-stakes Tax Maneuvering in 2012 Haunts Deliberations on Deficit." *Topeka Capital-Journal*, January 30.

Carpenter, Tim. 2018. "New GDP Index Shows Kansas Struggling to Keep Pace with Rival States." *The Topeka Capital-Journal*, January 28.

Chilson, Morgan. 2017. "Kansas Down 9,400 Private Sector Jobs in 2016." *The Topeka Capital-Journal*, January 20.

Hawver, Martin. 2017. *Highway Projects Shrink Away*. Hawver's Capitol Report, January 24.

Helling, Dave. 2017. "What Congress can Learn from Sam Brownback: Kansas Tax Cuts were Bad Policy and Bad Politics." *The Kansas City Star*, October 24.

Lowry, Brian. 2014. "S & P Downgrades Kansas Bond Rating; Brownback Pushes Back." *Wichita Eagle*, August 6.

Madden, Nathan. 2017. *Despite Promises, More Kansans Left the State after 2012 Income Tax Plan*. Kansas Center for Economic Growth, April 20. https://realprosperityks.com/.

Shorman, Jonathan. 2017. "KanCare Extension Denied after Scathing Review Finds Noncompliance with Federal Law." *Topeka Capital-Journal*, January 18.

Topeka Capital-Journal Editorial Board. 2018. "Time Right for Brownback to Move On." *The Topeka Capital-Journal*, January 26.

U.S. News and World Report. 2018. *Best States Rankings*. https://www.usnews.com/news/best-states/rankings.https://www.usnews.com/news/best-states/rankings.

Chapter 10

Afterword

Officially, Kansas' "Great Experiment" ended with the revenue bill passed in 2017. However, the state's budget woes remain ongoing. The state highway fund remains depleted, as do others, while still others were liquidated entirely (Carpenter 2017). The *Gannon* lawsuit over school funding remains current, with the Legislature still passing only temporary fixes (Lefler, Woodall, Bergen, and Tobias 2018). The privatized KanCare system remains as the state's approach to disbursing Medicaid. Newly elected governor Laura Kelly believes that Kansas must undo the "Experiment" as well as continuing to come to grips with the ongoing school funding issue and expanding Medicaid (Kelly 2019).

Not everyone is on board. Kelly's opponent, 2018 GOP Gubernatorial nominee Kris Kobach, rejected the idea that the Experiment was a mistake. He promised to do all he has to restore Brownback's policies if he won the governorship (Lefler 2018). Kobach was defeated by Kelly, a Democrat, 48 percent to 43 percent (there was also an independent candidate in the race). Yet, the Kansas Legislature actually moved to the right in these same elections. The conservatives gained seats at the expense of moderate Republicans in the house. As a result, moderate majority leader Don Hineman was ousted by conservative Dan Hawkins, who opposed Medicaid expansion (Shorman 2018).

In 2019, legislative leadership announced as their top priority, tax cuts to offset a $190 million tax "windfall" resulting from federal tax changes (Carpenter 2019). This is money that could instead address the state's school funding lawsuits, replenish trust funds, or fund Medicaid expansion, all without requiring the legislature to pass increases in tax rates. For their part, the Kansas Policy Institute argues that the state never seriously pursued offsetting the lost revenue with spending cuts (Trabert 2016). In particular, they continue to accuse schools of having bloated administrative expenses (Trabert 2018).

Critics of the Great Experiment often cite Kansas' woes as examples for other states. Goossen even traveled to Arizona in 2017, to encourage state legislators to resist Governor Ducey's call for similar cuts there (Pitzl 2017). In the end, the Republican-controlled Legislature did pass tax cuts, but scaled back substantially from the sweeping ones in Ducey's plan (Fischer 2017). In 2018, Arizona and Oklahoma both experienced widespread teacher strikes (Associated Press 2018; Goldstein and Dias 2018). The two states ranked very low compared to others, in terms of average teacher pay. Many observers attributed the two states' low teacher pay to tax cuts enacted earlier, before the Kansas Great Experiment (Leachman 2018).

The state most often compared to Kansas in regard to tax cuts was Louisiana (Greenblatt 2016). As governor, Bobby Jindal presided over a deep tax-cutting experiment similar to Brownback's—and with similar results. The two states are hardly identical. Both states have significant revenues from oil and gas, but considerably more in Louisiana. Yet the outcome of the two experiments was remarkably similar. Louisiana's started and ended a bit earlier, lasting from 2008 to 2016. The new governor, John Bel Edwards, spearheaded a successful bill to increase taxes. As of 2016, the state's budget shortfall had shrunk from $3 billion to $750 million. When Jindal had assumed office, the state had a $1 billion *surplus* (ibid.).

Supporters of the Great Experiment, including Brownback himself, often point to a different state. "Look out Texas, here comes Kansas," he famously said in his 2013 State of the State Address. Brownback was referencing Texas' combination of no income tax and economic growth that frequently exceeds the U.S. average. This trend has continued. An October 2018 report by the Federal Reserve Bank of Dallas, for example, shows that Texas' economy grew at 2.9 percent per quarter, versus 2.2 percent for the nation (Meier and Orrenius 2018). The Lone Star State also features the highest personal income growth in the nation—6 percent. Job growth also exceeds the national average—3 percent in Texas versus 1.7 percent nationally. It is not difficult to see why Brownback took this as his example for low taxes and rapid growth.

What went wrong? For one thing, Texas features some of America's largest, fastest-growing metropolitan areas. All in all, the state's population is nearly ten times that of Kansas and is still growing. Texas also has a different economic base. The Federal Reserve Bank of Dallas reports that Texas' robust export industry is easily led by petroleum and coal production—sectors that far outstrip their counterparts in Kansas. In addition, critics have noted that Texas' economy consists disproportionately of low-wage jobs. The state leads the nation by far in percentage of minimum wage workers (Schnurman 2019).

Second, low taxes come at a price. Texas' percentage of residents with no health insurance is 9 percent, well above the national average of 5 percent, which includes the nation's highest percentage of uninsured children. Nationally, one in five children lacking health coverage lives in Texas (Novack 2018).

Finally, Texas state finances are a mess (Collier 2018). The state's highway funds alone run a deficit of $4 billion per year (ibid.). By contrast, the Kansas highway trust fund was in surplus before the Brownback experiment. Texas' property taxes are the sixth highest in the nation (Alfonso 2019). Still the revenue is not enough: Texas school districts collectively pay over $6 billion per year in debt service, and Lt. Governor Dan Patrick's recent budget proposal included provisions to increase property taxes by 26.9 percent over the next four years (ibid.).

If there is any clear lesson from the comparison, it is that states lacking an income tax frequently are forced to offset it with cuts to government services, high debt, and high property taxes. It is less clear that Texas' economic growth is an example applicable to Kansas, given the state's huge population and heavy dependence on the oil and coal industries. Furthermore, resources, technology, and trade are important elements in economic growth; compared with Kansas, Texas has some obvious geographical advantages with its relatively warm climate and ports.

Journalist Alan Greenblatt suggested that the results of the Kansas and Louisiana experiments cooled "Tax Cut Fever" in other states—but not entirely. Two prominent states to pass tax cuts after the Experiment were Missouri and Iowa. However, there was some evidence of lessons learned, particularly regarding the so-called pay-fors, which had been stripped from the Kansas bill before Brownback signed it. In Missouri, which shares Kansas' most-populous border, Governor Mike Parson signed a bill lowering the top income tax rate from 5.8 percent to 5.4 percent (Wornell 2018). This followed an earlier bill lowering corporate tax rates. However, revenue targets must be met for the income tax rate to drop further to 5.1 percent in the future—and that is the final number; there is no "glide path to zero." The state estimated that the bill would mean a $5.8 million decrease, offset by a downward shift in tax bracket thresholds and a phase out on the deductibility of federal taxes (ibid.) One group even estimated that the tax changes would lead to *increased* revenue, on balance. Budget officials made it a point to contrast their cautious approach with the Kansas "glide path." Even the bill's sponsor, Rep. Elijah Haahr, said that "in Kansas, you had a full scale, almost elimination of the tax system. This is nothing like Kansas. We were very careful . . . " (ibid.).

Also in 2018, Iowa took a considerably bolder approach when Governor Kim Reynolds signed the largest tax cut in state history—estimated at $2.86

billion (Lynch 2018). The bill was controversial and passed without a single Democratic vote. However, it, too, contrasted with the Great Experiment. The bill was a one-time tax cut with no "glide path." It included pay-fors, primarily in the form of broadening the sales tax base to include online shopping, digital purchases, travel sites, subscription, and ride-hailing services, raising an estimated $725 million. This is well short of the revenue projected to be lost, however, leading critics to predict higher property taxes and college tuition (ibid.).

Finally, and most notably, there was the U.S. federal government. In 2017, Congress passed and President Trump signed a sweeping change to the U.S. tax code, including a lowering of the rate and raising of the threshold for the top tax bracket, a cut in the corporate income tax, and other changes (Long 2017). The bill was predicted to cost the feds $1.5 trillion in revenue (Bixby 2017). However, it, too, had significant differences from the Kansas approach. First, as in Missouri and Iowa, it was a one-time cut. There was no "glide path." Second, a pay-for was included in the form of caps on the deductibility of state, local, and property taxes. And finally, the income tax cuts in the bill included "sunset" provisions. Without additional action by Congress, the rates revert to the old, higher ones in 2026 (Long).

Perhaps Greenblatt is correct. Perhaps "Tax Cut Fever" has cooled due to the experiments in Kansas and Louisiana. The zeal of politicos—particularly Republicans—for cutting taxes certainly has not disappeared, and the federal government and Iowa now face substantial revenue shortfalls due to tax cuts that substantially exceeded their pay-fors. However, they did *include* pay-fors, unlike the bill signed by Brownback in 2014, which had them stripped away before final passage. For its part, the Arizona Legislature passed a tax increase to fund a promised increase to teacher pay (AP), while Oklahoma legislators appropriated money for the same and now must identify the revenue or depend on economic growth (Goldstein and Dias).

Perhaps most notable about these new tax cuts is that they do not include "glide paths." Missouri's cut to the top tax rate stops at 5.1 percent—and only gets there if revenue targets are met. Iowa and the federal government's cuts are one-time-only measures, and some of the largest federal cuts are sunset to 2026. Back in Kansas, the stage is set for a protracted battle between Governor Kelly and the conservative majorities in the Legislature.

REFERENCES

Alfonso, Fernando. 2019. "Texas' Property Tax Rate Among Highest In Nation." *Patch.com*, January 18. https://patch.com/texas/dallas-ftworth/texas-property-tax-rate-among-highest-nation.

Associated Press. 2018. "Striking Arizona Teachers with 19% Raise, End Walkout." *Los Angeles Times*, May 3.

Bixby, Robert L. 2017. "Tax Cut Numbers Don't Add Up." *The Concord Coalition*, November 20. https://www.concordcoalition.org/special-publication/tax-cut-numbers-dont-add.

Carpenter, Tim. 2017. "The Brownback Legacy: He Touts Pro-life Work; Skeptics Point to Damaging Tax Cuts." *The Topeka Capital-Journal*, July 30.

Carpenter, Tim. 2019. "Kansas Senate Advances $190 Million Tax 'Windfall' Bill Denounced by Gov. Laura Kelly." *Ottawa Herald*, February 6.

Collier, Mike. 2018. "Texas' Property Tax Mess." *The Texas Tribune*, July 23. https://www.tribtalk.org/2018/07/23/texas-property-tax-mess.

Fischer, Howard. 2017. "Arizona Legislature Ends Term by Passing Slew of Tax Breaks for Businesses." *Tucson.com,* May 10. https://tucson.com/news/local/arizona-legislature-ends-term-by-passing-slew-of-tax-breaks/article_5aa7e339-92e5-5236-a3ad-3eb065f7aafa.html.

Goldstein, Dana and Elizabeth Dias. 2018. "Oklahoma Teachers End Walkout After Winning Raises and Additional Funding." *New York Times*, April 12.

Greenblatt, Alan. 2016. "Why States' Tax-Cut Fever Has Subsided." *Governing.com*, June. http://www.governing.com/topics/finance/gov-tax-cut-states-republicans.html.

Kelly, Laura. 2019. "State of the State Address." January 16. https://governor.kansas.gov/governor-laura-kellys-state-of-the-state-address.

Leachman, Michael. 2018. *State Tax Cuts: A Key Factor in AZ, OK Teacher Pay Crises*. Center on Budget and Policy Priorities, March 26. https://www.cbpp.org/blog/state-tax-cuts-a-key-factor-in-az-ok-teacher-pay-crises.

Lefler, Dion. 2018. "Kobach Wants to Restore Brownback Tax Plan, Vows Never to Raise Taxes as Governor." *The Wichita Eagle*, April 17.

Lefler, Dion, Hunter Woodall, Katy Bergen, and Suzanne Tobias. 2018. "Kansas School Funding Still Inadequate, Supreme Court Says." *The Kansas City Star*, June 25.

Long, Heather. 2017. "The Final GOP Tax Bill Is Complete; Here's What Is In It." *Washington Post*, December 15.

Lynch, James Q. 2018. "Iowa Governor Signs Largest Tax Cut in State's History." *Governing.com,* June 1. http://www.governing.com/topics/finance/tns-iowa-tax-cut-reynolds.html.

Meier, Benjamin and Pia Orrenius. 2018. *Texas Economy Keeps Growing but Signs of Supply-Side Constraints Emerge*. Federal Reserve Bank of Dallas, October 3. https://www.dallasfed.org/research/update/reg/2018/1806.

Novack, Sophie. 2018. "Texas' Uninsured Rate for Kids, Highest in the Country, Increased for the First Time in Years." *The Texas Observer*. https://www.texasobserver.org/texas-uninsured-rate-for-kids-highest-in-the-country-increased-for-the-first-time-in-years.

Pitzl, Mary Jo. 2017. "A Warning to Arizona on Income Tax Cuts: 'Don't Do What Kansas Did.'" *Arizona Republic*, January 5.

Schnurman, Mitchell. 2019. "Another Texas Brag: We're Still No. 1 in Minimum-wage Workers (By Far)." *The Dallas Morning News* (online), January 6.

Shorman, Jonathan. 2018. "Kansas House Republicans Pick Conservative Leader Who Opposes Medicaid Expansion." *The Wichita Eagle*, December 3.

Trabert, Dave. 2016. *Houston, We Have a Spending Problem*. Kansas Policy Institute, February 20. https://kansaspolicy.org/houston-we-have-a-spending-problem.

Trabert, Dave. 2018. *Olathe School Administrators' Big Pay Hike Won't Help Students*. Kansas Policy Institute, July 26. https://kansaspolicy.org/olathe-school-administrators-big-pay-hike-wont-help-students.

Wornell, Tyler. 2018. "Despite Fears of Becoming Kansas, Missouri Cuts Taxes." *Governing.com*, July 16. http://www.governing.com/topics/finance/tns-missouri-tax-cut.html.

Appendix

Arthur Laffer's Sketch of Supply-Side Theory

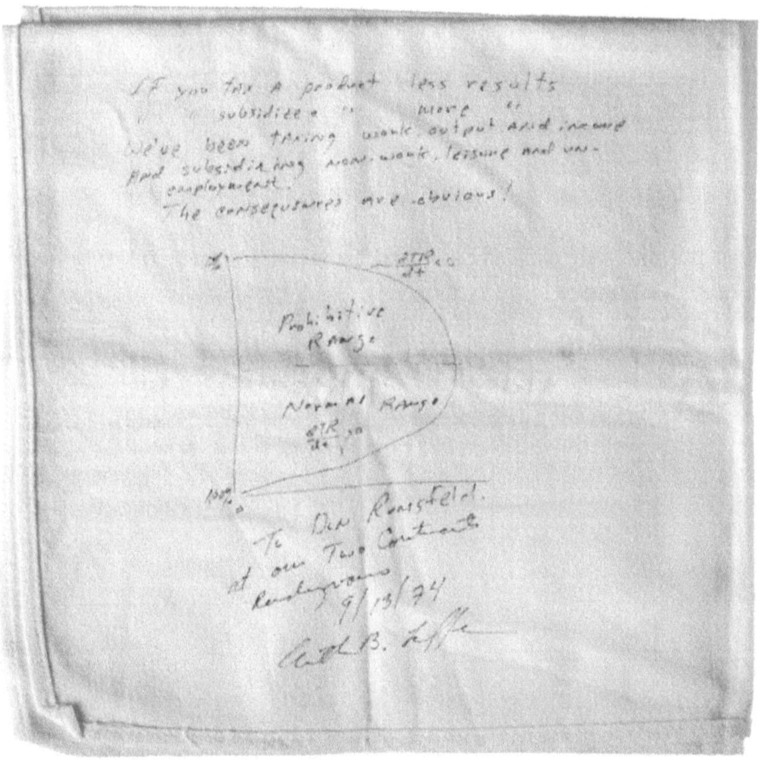

Figure A.1 Arthur Laffer's Sketch of Supply-Side Theory. *Source*: Division of Work and Industry, National Museum of American History, Smithsonian Institution.

Source: National Museum of American History. http://americanhistory.si.edu/collections/search/object/nmah_1439217

The interested reader might note some of the mathematical notation on the napkin. The top side of the Laffer Curve has something like the following:

$$\frac{dTR}{dt} < 0$$

where:
d = change
TR = Tax Revenue
t = tax rate
<0 indicates a negative value, which in this case is a negative slope.

Mathematically, this would be the first derivative of the tax revenue function with respect to the tax rate (*t*) and it is less than zero. This is likely intended to reinforce notion that the slope of the total tax revenue function as illustrated in Arthur Laffer's curve has a negative slope.

Similarly, the equation below the inscription "Normal Range" likely draws attention to the positive slope in the bottom half of the curve.

$$\frac{dTR}{dt} > 0$$

In less technical terms, it means that an increase in the tax rate in the bottom part of the Laffer Curve is likely to generate an increase in tax revenue.

Bibliography

Bartlett, Bruce R. 1981. *Reaganomics: Supply Side Economics in Action.* Westport, CN: Arlington House.

Brookes, Warren T. 1982. *The Economy in Mind.* New York: Universe Books.

Brownback, Sam. 2007. *From Power to Purpose.* Nashville, TN: Thomas Nelson.

Critchlow, D. T. 2011. *The Conservative Ascendancy: How the Republican Right Rose to Power in Modern America.* Lawrence, KS: University Press of Kansas.

Domitrovic, Brian. 2014. *The Pillars of Reaganomics.* San Francisco: Laffer Center at the Pacific Research Institute.

Frank, T. 2004. *What's the Matter With Kansas? How Conservatives Won the Heart of America.* New York: Henry Holt.

Greenstein, F. I. 1982. *The Hidden-Hand Presidency: Eisenhower As Leader.* Baltimore, MA: Basic Books.

Howard, P. K. 2011. *The Death of Common Sense: How Law Is Suffocating America.* New York: Random House.

Krugman, Paul R. 1994. *Peddling Prosperity: Economic Sense and Nonsense in the Age of Diminished Expectations.* New York: W.W. Norton.

Laffer, Arthur B. 2014. "Time Wounds All Heels, July 22, 1994." In *The Pillars of Reaganomics,* edited by Brian Domitrovic, 121–129. San Francisco: Laffer Center at the Pacific Research Institute.

Laffer, Arthur B., Stephen Moore, and Peter J. Tanous. 2008. *The End of Prosperity; How Higher Taxes Will Doom the Economy—If We Let It Happen.* New York: Threshold Editions.

Laffer, Arthur B., Stephen Moore, Rex A. Sinquefield, and Travis H. Brown. 2014. *An Inquiry into the Nature and Causes of the Wealth of States: How Taxes, Energy, and Worker Freedom Change Everything.* Hoboken, NJ: Wiley.

Loomis, B. A. 1993. *Time, Politics, and Policies.* Lawrence, KS: University Press of Kansas.

Mellon, Andrew W. 1924. *Taxation, the People's Business.* New York: Macmillan.

Perlstein, Rick. 2008. *Nixonland: The Rise of a President and the Fracturing of America.* New York: Scribner.

Perlstein, R. 2009. *Before The Storm: Barry Goldwater and the Unmaking of the American Consensus.* New York: Nation Books.

Perlstein, R. 2014. *The Invisible Bridge: The Fall of Nixon and The Rise of Reagan.* New York: Simon & Schuster.

Pierce, Neal R. and Jerry Hagstrom. 1983. *The Book of America: Inside the 50 States Today.* New York: Warner Books.

Wanniski, Jude. 1978. "Taxes, Revenues, and the 'Laffer Curve.'" *The Public Interest*, Winter 1978.

Wanniski, Jude. 1978. *The Way the World Works: How Economies Fail—And Succeed.* New York: Basic Books.

Index

About the Authors

Rob Catlett thoroughly enjoys teaching a variety of undergraduate and graduate courses in economics in the Department of Mathematics and Economics at Emporia State University (ESU). In addition to dozens of refereed journal articles in economics, many of which are in economic conditions analysis, Rob is active in a variety of local, regional, and national organizations. He is Director, ESU Centers for Economic Education and Community Research and immediate Past President of the Faculty at ESU, and he has served on boards, councils, and executive committees for a variety of organizations ranging from the national American Democracy Project to the Federal Reserve Bank of Kansas City. Rob is a native of Colorado and lived in Wyoming and Nebraska prior to moving to Kansas, where he has been an economics professor for over forty years.

Robert J. Grover is a retired university administrator and professor emeritus in the School of Library and Information Management at Emporia State University. He previously taught at University of South Florida and University of Southern California. He has authored numerous refereed journal articles and book chapters. More recent books that he has coauthored include *Helping Those Experiencing Loss: A Guide to Grieving Resources* (2011); *Introduction to the Library and Information Professions* (2007, 2013); *Evolving Global Information Infrastructure and Information Transfer* (2015); and *Libraries Partnering with Self-Publishing: A Winning Combination* (2016), all published by Libraries Unlimited. A native Hoosier, Bob has been a Kansas resident and follower of Kansas politics for 35 years.

Michael A. Smith is a professor of political science and Chair of Social Sciences at Emporia State University. He has also taught at the University of Kansas, Kansas State University, Iowa State University, and Millikin University. Prior to this book, Smith's most recent book project was *State Voting Laws in America* (w/Chapman Rackaway and Kevin Anderson, Palgrave Pivot, 2015). He has also published *Bringing Representation Home: State Legislators Among Their Constituencies* (Missouri, 2003) and numerous peer-reviewed articles. Smith writes a monthly newspaper column for the Insight Kansas group, blogs for the Midwest Political Science Association, and is regularly quoted in newspapers, radio, and television, analyzing Kansas politics.

www.ingramcontent.com/pod-product-compliance
Ingram Content Group UK Ltd.
Pitfield, Milton Keynes, MK11 3LW, UK
UKHW041123071026
15587UKWH00009B/122